GOD'S PLAN

LEGACY
press

Published by Legacy Press

Copyright © 2020 by Douglas W. Reynolds

For permission, please write to dwr61315@gmail.com.

Printed in the United States of America

Library of Congress Control Number:

ISBN (softcover):   978-1-7342435-0-5
ISBN (ebook):   978-1-7342435-1-2

Available from Amazon.com and other retail outlets.

Cover design, interior design and layout by
Nelly Murariu @PixBeeDesign.com

GOD'S PLAN

From Glitz and Glory
To the
Peace of God

DOUGLAS W. REYNOLDS
WITH ROBIN GRUNDER

To My Donna

From the day we met and every day since, your quiet confidence, happiness, kindness and lack of worry have both intrigued and inspired me. I didn't know then what gave you this peace, but I did know that I wanted to have what you had. Thank you for introducing me to the giver of true peace and happiness, Jesus Christ.

To My Creator, Jesus

Thank you for the wonderful life and amazing experiences you have given me. But mostly, thank you for the abundant life and peace that comes from acknowledging, knowing, and following you. I pray you will use the words of my story to bring others to know this abundance and peace you have given me.

Acknowledgements

It is one thing to want to write a book, and quite another to actually do it. I owe a gratitude of thanks to those who helped me see this undertaking through, from my first thoughts of starting such a project, to the completion of a published book.

Matt Loehr:

You were the first person I came to on this pilgrimage of writing a book. Thank you for your encouragement and for helping me understand the first steps I needed to take in writing a book. I also thank you for leading me to find a ghostwriter.

Robin Grunder:

You sat through hours of interview sessions, listening to my stories, and helping me to stay on track. Somehow, you were able to take my jumbled thoughts and weave them together, creating a narrative of some of my life-stories. Thank you for writing my story in a way that kept me focused on the most important thread of all—my story of faith. I also thank you for pointing me in the right direction to see that my book was published.

Renee Fisher:

You have spent so much time corresponding back and forth with me and walking me through the publishing process. Thank you for taking the time to understand my vision, for your patience with me, and for bringing my vision for a published book to life.

Contents

Prologue   xi

Chapter One: Childhood Memories and Reflections   1

Chapter Two: Boyhood to Manhood   13

Chapter Three: Then I Met Her   21

Chapter Four: Reynolds Motor Company; DBA Reynold's Ford   31

Chapter Five: Our Journey to Success   43

Chapter Six: Glitz, Glory, and a Carefree Life   51

Chapter Seven: Troubled Waters   65

Chapter Eight: Handing Over the Baton   71

Chapter Nine: God Sent Me an Angel   75

Chapter Ten: My Donna   81

Chapter Eleven: Spiritual Awakening   93

Epilogue   97

Blessings   99

About the Author   104

Prologue

I'VE WRITTEN MY OWN OBITUARY. It includes all the normal things; when and where I was born, who my parents were, the people in my family who have passed before me, and the people who I am survived by. I included my own version of a highlight reel of my life; major accomplishments, awards, organizations I've been involved with, and a whole slew of positive things that I have done in the community and the various ways I am recognized. Besides what I have written about myself in my obituary, I attached some statements of nice things that others whom I would consider people of influence have said about me, my life, and all the good I have done.

I realize what I just admitted may come off as prideful. Perhaps even conceited. The words I wrote in my obituary are the things I want people to know about me, and how I hope to be remembered. That is what I believed, anyway. But not so much anymore.

The only things I don't have written in my obituary are my date of death. And how this particular day will be the start of my eternal life in heaven.

Other things you won't find in my obituary include things I regret; the ways I've failed—both myself and my family. Things that are uncomfortable to talk about. Things that would paint me in a negative light. Not that it will matter when I am gone from this world, but the fear of rejection or having the regrets overshadow the successes weigh on my heart. And yet, now that I've been able to take a look at my life in hindsight, I realize that perhaps my biggest failure is not talking about the things I regret.

A man my age has many of those.

Undoubtedly, the biggest regret I have is that I never told my children that I loved them. Hopefully by the time this is published, that will have changed.

I don't understand why I didn't say those words, because I always have and always will love my children. Perhaps it was because I never heard those words from my own parents. Maybe they never heard it either, I really don't know. How do you do something you didn't know you were supposed to do?

But now I know.

I've decided to write this book as a way to share some of my life-story. There is no arguing that I've had a good one. I have had so many unique opportunities throughout my entire life that most people never have the chance to experience.

The obituary I wrote is true. I've worked hard, experienced great success, and have been able to contribute to the betterment of the community I live in. I spent nearly my whole life taking it by the horns and tackling each day with my own purpose and expectations in mind. I've strived and achieved. I've overcome many obstacles, and sometimes, things just came extremely natural to me. My life has been good. That is how I used to look at life. Mine.

You will read about these things in the following pages, and it has been a good experience for me to relive some of the memories by writing them down. Especially in hindsight. And through the lens of faith.

I recognize that all the good that has come to me was not because of me at all. Not my efforts in striving for success, or anything of my own doing. God simply blessed me with a life that I still cannot believe I've been given. He has given me so many good things.

I also write about some of the low parts of life. The struggles of losing babies, being a caregiver for a spouse who passed away, the grief, and yes, the regrets. I think if I'm really going to share who Doug Reynolds is, I need to let you in on these things as well.

But even as I share the low points, I can look back and see how God had a plan in and through those times. He's always had a plan.

I believe He has a plan for this book I'm writing. When I have passed from this life into the gates of heaven, I will know that my family was well cared for financially. But I want more for them. I want my children, grandchildren, and great-grandchildren to know where they came from. I want them to know who I am so that they can perhaps better understand who they are. I want them to know that they can overcome obstacles and achieve great things.

The words written in my obituary are not my ultimate legacy. The inheritance I leave behind is not my ultimate legacy.

I want to leave behind a legacy of faith.

It is my hope that as you get to know me through the stories I share, you'll also get to know a little more about the God I believe in. It took many decades before I could see how God has intervened in my life from the very beginning, but now that I know it, I owe it to you to share.

Because if I don't, I know I'll regret it.

DOUG REYNOLDS

Even when I am old and gray,
Do not forsake me, my God,
till I declare your power to
the next generation,
your mighty acts to all
who are to come.

Psalm 71:18 (NIV)

CHAPTER ONE

Childhood Memories and Reflections

MY FATHER, ERDIE, grew up on a farm in Wisconsin. He had to quit school to work full-time on the farm in seventh grade, when his own father died.

My father once told me how he had been an athlete when he was younger, especially in when it came to playing football. Unfortunately, an injury to his back during practice or a game ended his time playing the sport. When his back was hurting, he was not able to complete his chores. My grandfather burned my father's uniform and said, "Now go do your chores."

By the time Erdie was seventeen, he came to realize that there would be no future as far as making a decent living working on the farm. He left home and became a lineman for Western Electric. His work took him all across the country, traveling from New York to San Francisco.

Even at the new job, the old football injury would catch up to my father. When he traveled through Davenport with Western Electric, he heard about Palmer School of Chiropractic and how they might be able to help his back. He went to a chiropractor and indeed, they fixed his back. This was such a turning

ERDIE REYNOLDS

point for my father that he decided he wanted to become a chiropractor and help other people.

With no means to pay for schooling or support himself, Erdie answered an ad for a Ford salesman position in Rock Island. He applied for and got the job, became an instant success, and moved into a sales manager position. Soon after, he went on to manage the Ford dealership in Moline, Illinois, all while attending classes and graduating from Palmer College of Chiropractic.

Dad did so well in management with this Ford dealer that he came to the notion that maybe he should be working for himself. When he had this conversation with the owner about wanting to quit and become a Ford dealer, he learned that he didn't have enough money to buy his own dealership. The dealer, M. E. Strieter, set him up with a buyout arrangement at Horst-Strieter in East Moline in 1925. Five years later, the buyout was complete and became Reynolds Motor Company.

The timing of the buyout came just when the depression hit. The war then followed. It was not a good time to be selling cars. Car manufacturers were focused on producing military vehicles.

However, dad had already become a chiropractor. He was able to keep the dealership afloat by seeing patients out of his home over the noon hour and then again in the evenings. Some people might call this a great coincidence. I look back and see this as the work of God. I remember dad once telling me that at one point in his career, he could have made more money as a chiropractor than he did as a Ford Dealer. He genuinely loved both.

When I was a kid, I remember a young man who came to him on crutches. My dad helped him, and he was eventually drafted to do some kind of office work in the war. There were a lot of people that came in all bent over and would walk right back out standing straight. Once I had an earache and my father gave me a chiropractic adjustment. It went away immediately. To this day, I believe chiropractic has its benefits for many things.

My mom, Lydia, grew up in Des Moines. She had one sister. Her father passed away when she was eleven, and her mother scrimped and saved to put both girls through college.

LYDIA REYNOLDS

I believe my mom was very social and had a gift for music and singing. When she graduated from college, she moved to Davenport to take a teaching position, but she would still sing at weddings and other functions.

Somehow, her voice got "caught" and she wasn't able to sing. She ended up visiting a chiropractor and the problem was cured.

That is how my parents met and were married. Their ceremony took place in the Little Brown Church in Nashua, Iowa, made famous by the song "The Little Brown Church in the Vale" written by William Pitts, and later performed by the Statler Brothers. My wife and I recently visited this church and I have included a photo from that day. My parents had my sister Ramona and me. When Ramona attended college at the University of Illinois, she contracted mononucleosis.

My parents took her to Florida to recuperate. Later she married Clifford Zude and finished college with a degree. They had two sons, Dale and Dan, who are both successful in their own careers.

My parents were liked by everyone we knew. They had personalities that people were naturally attracted to. But I don't know that I ever felt particularly close to my parents. My dad worked all the time and he enjoyed things like hunting and fishing. I know he wanted me to try the things that he liked, so one day I went out to shoot a rabbit in the backyard. I closed the wrong eye and missed it. That was the last of the BB guns.

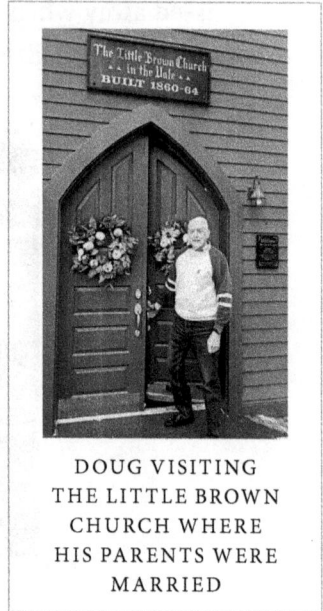

DOUG VISITING THE LITTLE BROWN CHURCH WHERE HIS PARENTS WERE MARRIED

He also took me fishing. I just didn't enjoy it. I was far more into sports and wanted activity. I wanted to outdo somebody and compete, not sit there in a boat and wait for a fish to come along. Once in high school, dad took me on a fishing trip. It ended up raining one of the days and he asked me if I wanted to go into town and play pool. I liked playing pool and would often play against my buddy John Campbell at his house. I thought I was pretty good. My father, on the other hand, had not played pool for forty years. On that day, I saw him taking shots that I had never seen before. I was lucky to beat him by one ball. That was the highlight of the whole fishing trip for me.

My parents hardly saw me play basketball. My father went once when I was in grade school. I hate to admit it, but he was the only person wearing a suit in the audience. Everyone else worked in a factory. They never came to see me play tennis.

I think they were proud of me. They seemed to support me. But that never translated to spending time with me. I never felt a closeness with them. And like I said before, they never told me they loved me.

This undoubtedly translated into how I parented. I know this probably isn't the best way to illustrate my point, but I liken it to how I learned to train dogs. If the dog went in the house, I was taught to punish the pet by hitting it on the butt and say "NO-NO!" When I did this with a rescue dog, my methods did not work. It was the exact opposite of giving the dog confidence, and he actually came after me three times. I learned with this dog that I had to discipline with love and affection. Now every time the dog sees me, he knows that I love him and he reciprocates.

I'm not a dog and neither are my children. My point is that I just didn't know that I should have been telling them I love them all along. My old ways of doing things, the ways I thought I was showing love and support—trying to coach them, provide for them, push them to do things I thought they could do—did not translate into giving them confidence. It definitely was not the same as saying "I love you," and then stepping back. It's not an excuse, just an explanation. I did what I thought I should do, what I saw my parents do, and now that I look back on my own life and my relationship with them, I realize that my ways of wanting to connect, support, and love my children probably left them with the same feelings that I now have about my relationship with my own parents.

I regret that. I can't change the past. But I intend on not letting any excuse or explanation get in the way as I move forward.

Don't get me wrong. I liked my parents. I'd like to say that I'm similar to my parents in the way that people generally liked them. I like being around people and I think people like me. It's not something I have to work at. It comes naturally.

Having said all of that, I truly did have a happy childhood. My sister Ramona and I have many fond memories of growing up and me being able to play in the woods, playing with frogs and all kinds of animals. I've always had a dog. I did while I was growing up and I do now. There's something to be said about dogs being "man's best friend" and the unconditional love they show.

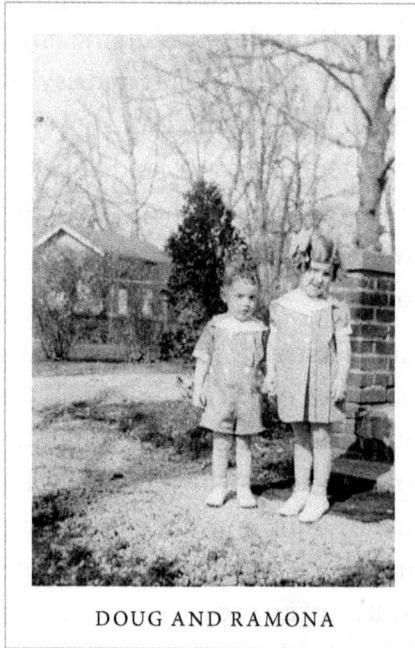

DOUG AND RAMONA

I grew up during a time when I could be out riding my bike until the streetlights came on. The neighborhood kids were close to my age and we didn't require any supervision, or it wasn't really something that was thought of. We played baseball, ran around, and rode bikes.

Sometimes when I was around eight or nine, I became friends with one of our neighbors' nephews. One day we went up to the football field. The field was closed and there were two ticket windows. We were playing "army" and thought it would be fun to throw rocks through the ticket windows like they were hand grenades and climb in through them. It was innocent play, but destructive, nonetheless. We didn't steal anything; we were only trying to conquer something in our play.

We left and I don't remember if I actually told my mother that we had been playing around the football field, but somehow, they found out that I was probably the one who broke the windows. Boy did they teach me a lesson. One day soon after we had broken the windows, I was playing in the basement and my mother calls down and said that someone was there to see me. I went to the front door and there stood a policeman. He walked me out and told me he wanted to take me to the station for questioning. I was placed in the backseat of the police car, where I slumped down because I was scared to death and I didn't want anyone to see me.

I knew what I had done and why they were going to question me. But when we got to the station and they asked, "Did you do that?" I emphatically denied having any part of it. "OH, NO!" I kept on saying. Then they changed tactics and informed me that my buddy told them that he did it and I was there. As soon as they said that, I admitted, "I did it."

It's a funny story to me today and I still laugh when I think about it. But boy, back then, it sure did make a significant impression on me. I would never wear the shirt I had on that day I spent at the police station ever again. I learned my lesson.

A fond memory I have of my childhood has to do with pigeons. Ironically, this story starts out with a rock as well! Around the fifth grade, I remember visiting some extended family for a weekend on their farm in Washington, Iowa. I was out in one of their barns and saw a pigeon up in the rafters. I took a rock and threw it up at the rafters towards the pigeon and hit him in the head. He came tumbling down and fell to the floor. I picked it up and held him. They asked me if I wanted to keep him and I did. They put the bird in a cardboard box, and I took him home with me.

That pigeon stayed on the stoop above the backdoor of our house and I fed it every day. I became fascinated with my bird and pigeons in general.

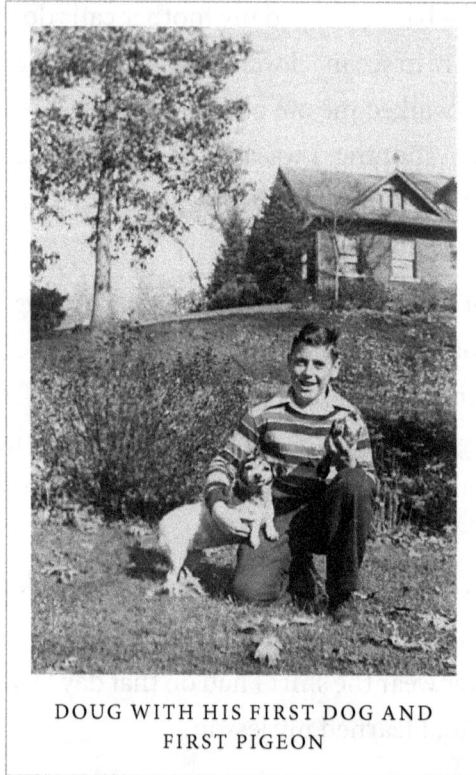

DOUG WITH HIS FIRST DOG AND
FIRST PIGEON

At that time, East Moline had a large Belgium population that held pigeon races all the time. I became enamored in learning about this, so my father introduced me to someone he knew who had a pigeon coop and gave me some young birds. We built a chicken wire cage in our basement where I would feed them.

There was an alley from 13th to 16th Street in East Moline where almost every house had a pigeon loft. I would walk that alley and look at those birds and talk to the old Belgium men that had them. They would invite me up into their coop. All the old guys chewed snuff and would spit. I would buy my own nips, put it in my mouth and spit that black stuff out just like they did.

I just loved the pigeons. I would take them to school for show-and-tell and watch them fly and tumble when I was going to or from school. I had this whistle and I would fantasize that I was calling my pigeons. I cleaned their coop and took care of watering and feeding them.

I was all into these birds and I wanted to see if I could race them like the Belgium men did. This sport involved putting a metal band on their leg when they are young in order to identify your own birds in the East Moline club. When training the birds, I learned to take them out and let them fly back a short distance. Then you would keep extending that distance. The Belgiums had these big wicker crates with little compartments. On Sundays, people would bring their birds that were placed in the crates, drive out to a certain location, and then release all the birds at once. The pigeons circle around until they get their bearings, then one bird will peel off, and then another, and another, until they all took off. At each loft, the people who are racing have a clock with a time stamp on it. The pigeons that raced all had a rubber band around their foot and when your pigeon comes home, you take that off and stamp it in the clock. If you had more than one bird, you would keep doing this as they all came in. Then each person who has birds in the race would go down to the local pigeon club and the winners would receive money and recognition. I found the whole thing really fascinating.

I went as far as Muscatine with my pigeons. I was just this young kid doing it on my own, so my dad would take me out there and we let the birds go and drove home. I never had any problems with the birds coming home when it was only a few miles or so. But when I extended the distance to Muscatine, it took two weeks for my birds to get home! One of the older fellas who raced birds spit and laughed as he stuttered, "Hey kid, I think your birds walked home!" It was funny, but the comment hurt because I wanted to be like the other pigeon owners.

OUTSIDE THE PIGEON COOP

I didn't know any other kids who did this with pigeons. All of the fellas I walked the street with who had birds were elderly. Pigeons were used in the war to deliver messages. They are a very unusual animal. Some of them fly an unheard-of number of miles to go home. Today it seems like taking care of and racing pigeons is becoming a dying hobby. I know there are still clubs around, but it certainly isn't as popular.

Something about sharing this story about pigeons and going home makes me think about my life and finding my way home. I've been flying around life, going from one activity, goal, or achievement to the next. I didn't always know where I was supposed to go, but I never stopped moving forward and reaching for the next big accomplishment. I did this with every organization I was involved in.

It has taken me awhile to find my bearings, and by that, I mean a faith in God and where my true home is; but I now know. My eternal home is in heaven. It doesn't matter how far away from faith I have been; I know where I'm going.

I want my family to know this about me, and hopefully have this homing pigeon faith.

**Some things I remember
from my elementary school years.**

I played the trumpet in the band

I was the center on the basketball team

In track and field, I participated in
the high jump and threw the shot put

I worked every summer at the dealership
from eighth grade on

CHAPTER TWO

Boyhood to Manhood

I HAD PIGEONS for quite a while, but I got rid of them when I went to high school and started getting more interested in sports, band, and girls. Not always in that order.

My mother made me take piano lessons when I was in grade school. I was terrible at it. I also learned to play the trumpet, and in high school, our assistant band director formed a dance band and we played at another school's prom. I laugh when I share this because we only had one gig, but it was a fun experience. My high school girlfriend was a vocalist. I was second chair in trumpet.

As a Freshman, I was some kind of class officer—I don't remember which one! I was also a part of the Spanish Club, and in a couple of plays. There was one play that I remembered all of my lines, and I can recall them to this day! The first line: "No, Tony." Then later in the play: "Sure." Another memory I laugh about!

Athletics really took over for me in high school. It was a way that I could become like everybody else and not just be the "rich kid." I don't know if it was necessarily true that our family was rich, but compared to a lot of others, it probably was. I know that my own kids went through a little of that, but I don't think it was quite as bad.

My mother had played some tennis when she was young, and she bought me a racket. I was also involved in basketball and was the center on the team up through the eighth grade. I wanted to play football, but my father would not let me go out because of how he had hurt his back when he played. I still wanted to be associated with the sport, so I joined as the equipment manager for the team. I also threw the shot put and high jump on the track team.

HIGH SCHOOL BASKETBALL

Tennis was my strong sport. I did play baseball, but the baseball and tennis seasons were at the same time, so it was easy to eliminate baseball. When I went to high school, I made the tennis team as their third-place person. For a Freshman, this was a pretty big achievement. Tennis didn't have a bad stigma nor was it seen as a sissy sport in East Moline. As a matter of fact, the number one tennis player on the team also played basketball and was the quarterback on the football team.

I worked my way up to be the number one tennis player on the team. We played against Moline and Davenport (back when Davenport was only one school) at Credit Island. I played as the number three player and beat my opponent. I remember that I jumped into the river to cool off and later thought it was kind of dumb. When I was the number one player on the team, we played Moline who was considered the local big powerhouse in tennis. I was the only East Moline player to win a match.

HIGH SCHOOL TENNIS TEAM

After practicing tennis, I had to walk past the field where the track kids were practicing. My junior varsity basketball coach was also the head track coach. On one occasion as I was walking from my practice and past theirs, I saw my basketball coach trying to teach the high jump. Me, being a smart-ass kid, I thought I could jump it. So I ran through their practice area, scissor-stepped it, and jumped. The coach called me over.

"Ya, coach?" I said. He instructed me that I was going to be their track team's high jumper. I insisted that I couldn't because I played tennis. He didn't ask me, but rather told me that after I was done with tennis practice, I would report to him and he would teach me the Western Roll in the high jump. So that is what I did.

I had never been out for track in high school. At my first meet I ended up with a third-place ribbon in the high jump. I was happy with that because I had never done it before, and my coach was elated because I earned points for the team. After I finished the high jump, my coach told me that I had to run a 400-meter leg in one of the races. I had never done this either. I started out my leg thinking that it wasn't too tough. I got ahead of the other guys until about a quarter of the way around the track. The others all started passing me and I thought I wasn't going to make it. My legs were like rubber. I ended up finishing and got a ribbon. There were five places and we got fifth. The coach didn't care because it still earned the team points that they otherwise wouldn't have had there not been someone to run it.

I was pretty confident when it came to sports. I found a lot of acceptance when I competed, and I always would do whatever the coach would ask of me.

This reminds me of when I taught my own kids to play tennis. They both made the team in high school. I remember watching my daughter play and I would later tell her that she should have done this or that. Instead of taking that as constructive criticism or helpful, she internalized it as hurtful and felt like she wasn't good enough. I never meant it that way at all, so I didn't understand her reaction at the time. Sherri did go on to coach, play, and place third nationally with a young lady in the Special Olympics. I hope that my daughter is able, in hindsight, to see that me pushing her was not about not being good enough. In fact, the way I intended my "coaching" to be was because I knew she was good enough.

The summer before high school I wanted to work. My father didn't want me to, so I applied for a job at a nearby feedstore. The guy who owned that store called my dad and said, "What's the matter Reynolds, won't you give your kid a job?" That evening my Dad said to me, "So you wanna go to work, huh?" He informed me that the owner of the feed mill called him, and I confirmed it. Dad said, "Okay then, pick up that broom."

My first job was sweeping floors.

FIRST JOB IN EIGHTH GRADE

I dated a couple of girls in high school. My first girlfriend and I started dating probably around the second semester of my Freshman year, through some time either Junior or Senior year. We had gone down to Lake Story in Galesburg and somebody bet me that I couldn't swim across the lake. I did. There were a bunch of people waiting for me. I thought they were going to tell me what a great job I did. Instead, I found out these people were officials and were shouting at me to get out of the lake and go home. "What do you think those barriers are for? We can't rescue you that far out!"

That was the night that my first girlfriend broke up with me. I was devastated.

I started dating a different girl for a short time. Then my first girlfriend and I began seeing each other again after playing in a band at a prom together. We dated until I met my first wife. I broke up with her on a weekend that I knew we would both be home from college. I know she went on to marry and have children. I also heard that she had become religious and wrote a book. I'm embarrassed to say that at our 50-year class reunion, I didn't recognize her. I should have.

In 8th grade, I had a Cushman Motor Scooter. I was 14 when I started driving this mini-motorcycle back and forth to work. My Freshman year, I got my first car, a Crosley Station Wagon. The fastest it would go is 60 mph, and that was downhill! One day my Freshman year, I came out of the school to the parking lot, got in it, started it up, and the wheels just spun and spun without going anywhere. My buddies stood by and laughed. The car was so light that they picked it up and put blocks under it. I pushed it off the blocks and drove home.

My next car was a 1937 Ford 2-door. My dad didn't think I needed a car because my parents thought I could just drive theirs. But I wanted my own car. One Sunday, my dad took me to the dealership and in the back was a black, 2-door 1937 Ford. It was exactly what I wanted.

A farmer had traded it in. He had seat covers on the seats and when we took them off, the seats looked brand new. This car was a '37 and the year I got it was 1950. It was black with yellow wheels. I did some drag racing and other stupid things like that. One time my friend John and I picked up a beggar, gave him a buck and dropped him off. The heater didn't have fresh-air heat, so the windows would steam up when you had the heater on. You had to wipe the windows on the inside. Back then, you could crank the windshield out for fresh air. I loved that car. I had it until I went to college. I drove into Champaign, Illinois in a brand-new red convertible with the top down and the radio up. I sure did think I was king of the walk driving through town, looking for girls as if to say, "Here I am!" It's bad, but true.

BRAND-NEW, RED CONVERTIBLE

High School Memories

Played the trumpet in the marching band, in a dance band, for high school prom, and played Taps at a veteran's funeral

Played basketball for four years

Played tennis for four years; was the number one player for two years

High Jump in track

Ran 400-meter leg of the 4x400 relay

Participated in school plays

CHAPTER THREE
Then I Met Her

I STARTED COLLEGE at the University of Illinois with the idea that I wanted to become a dentist. I finished college five years later at Millikin University in Decatur, Illinois with a Bachelor of Science degree in Merchandising. I learned quite a bit in college, mostly about myself.

Much like the rest of my life, I feel like a lot of unusual opportunities just "came" to me while I was in college. One example was through a PE course in fencing at the University of Illinois. While in this class, the instructor told me I should try out for the team. I ended up making the team. It is the most intricate sport I've ever participated in and I enjoyed the experience. It was also great to think that I was earning a "sweater with numerals" from a Big Ten School.

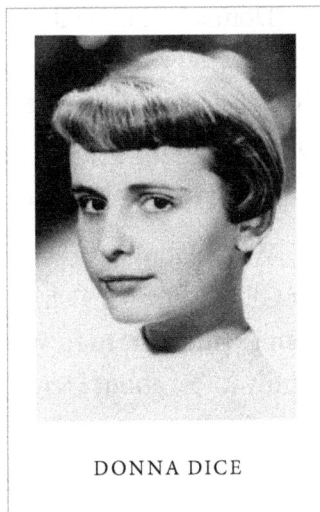

DONNA DICE

I dated while I was in college. I probably spent more time studying girls and fencing than my actual class work. One of my buddies fixed me up with a gal who lived in the same sorority house as his girlfriend. We had fun, but we both knew there wasn't a future there. I was looking for someone to be my girlfriend and not just a date. That's when I met Donna Dice.

We were both taking a Spanish course. She sat three seats down from me. I noticed that she was cute the minute I walked into the room. One day we were both asked to come to the blackboard to do an exercise on conjugating verbs or something like that. I kind of talked to her when we were up there. Each day I tried to talk to her a little bit more. I was looking for a way to ask her out.

I found out that she lived in the very same house as my fraternity brother's girlfriend and that first girl he had set me up with. Back in those days, there was a Greek life rule that states you were not allowed to date somebody new from the same house for a certain amount of time, so you wouldn't just be bouncing around from girl-to-girl. I really wanted to date Donna, so I asked the first girl that I went out with if she minded. We both had a good time, but neither of us wanted a relationship, so she gave her okay.

That is when I began dating Donna. She would later become my wife.

Donna introduced me to an entirely new world. She was from a big city, was very intelligent, and she was sure to let me know right away that I *was not* the greatest thing to walk the earth. She wasn't afraid to put me in my place.

Interestingly, Donna also had a background that tied in with Ford.

When Donna was a child, her father, Don, worked as an office boy for GE in Detroit, Michigan. Their family rented a house with another couple, and that man worked for Ford Motor Company. This other family knew about Henry Ford's private school that was rather exclusive. The learning and teaching models were somewhat experimental at the time. Henry Ford believed that if he were to put rich, middle class, and poor people together in an exclusive learning environment, they would all get along, everyone would learn from each other, and it would solve a great many problems of the world. You had to be invited to attend this school, which Ford named Greenfield Village. The students there had unlimited opportunities.

Anyway, the man that Donna's family rented a house from worked at Ford and they were able to get Donna into Greenfield Village. The couple who shared the house with them also worked for Ford and he eventually went on to become a big name at Ford Motor Company. Donna's dad eventually also became a big name with GE. The families became life-long friends.

As an "office boy" in Detroit, Don was made fun of a lot. I remember hearing a story about a summer when his co-workers sent him out to bring in ice to keep the office cool. By the time Don returned to the office, the ice had melted all over him. He put up with being the low man on the totem pole for a while. He learned and grew from his time in Detroit, but he certainly did not remain at the bottom of the totem pole. Don ended up moving up and on to become the head of the lamp division of GE in Chicago.

Donna attended high school in Chicago. She told me that one of her classmates was Marylyn Novak, who later became an actress by the name of Kim Novak. Kim and Jeanie Woodward went out to Hollywood together. Jeanie would land minor roles. "Kim" ended up making it pretty big.

Donna had to take a city bus in order to get to high school. She kept getting inappropriate propositions on the bus, so her dad decided to move to a suburb, where she was then able to attend a very affluent school. She didn't make many friends at this school. The girls didn't like her because the boys were all enticed by her. But Donna continued to propel herself intellectually.

When she graduated from high school, her plan was to go to college somewhere out East. But in the upcoming year, Illinois was supposed to play in the Rose Bowl, and her father tried to play that up. Don wasn't interested in paying the high tuition prices of the schools she was interested in. When they talked about the Rose Bowl, Donna must have agreed because that same day, her dad drove her to Illinois to register for classes. I suppose he didn't want to give her a chance to change her mind.

Donna's dad made around $10-12,000 while working in Chicago. That was considered pretty decent pay in the 1950s. But when he got an offer from C.M. Hall Lamp Company to take over the vice president position back in Detroit, which came with a significant increase in pay, it was something he could not pass up. The income allowed their family to experience a whole new lifestyle until the company was bought out. When Don lost his job, he went back to GE to see if they would hire him on again. GE must have thought a great deal of Don. Not only did he get his job back, but he received all of his pension as if he had never left. He was transferred to Philadelphia and became The Eastern Branch Marketing Coordinator. Don was wildly successful, moving up to a marketing management position of a new, numerical control plant in Virginia. He was credited for opening offices in Japan, Europe, and the United States. Upon his retirement, Don was honored by the Numerical Control Industry as "Mr. NC." He sold more numerical control industry machines than anyone in the entire world.

It's fair to say that Donna grew up with all the privileges that came with her family having money, connections, and the glitz of big city life in general.

Another fun fact about my years in college came with being a part of the ROTC. Back then, if you were a Freshman or Sophomore in college, you had to enroll in the ROTC. You could pick which branch—Army, Air Force, or Navy. I thought I wanted to be a dentist, so it really didn't matter to me. I went to the one with the shortest line—Army.

It might not seem like I always followed the rules, but in the ROTC, I did. My shoes were always polished, and I liked to be a part of anything that seemed spit and polish. I took classes on weapons and learned how to take them apart and put them back together. It

THREE: THEN I MET HER

was all basic stuff that everyone had to learn. My captain must have liked me. One day in class he told me I was "Point material," and that I should go to West Point.

I thought about that, as well as possibly joining the service and getting paid. But I found out that you couldn't be married if you went to West Point, and I knew that I wanted to marry Donna. Donna was worried I would get shot if I joined the service, so I stayed where I was for the time being.

Another memory about the ROTC has to do with the Military Ball. Only those who were in advanced, meaning they had committed to serving and becoming an officer after college, or the officials with all the brass, were allowed to attend the Ball.

The Military Ball produced a program for the dinner and dance and there was a competition for designing them. I submitted a design and ended up winning. In return, I was invited to attend the Ball even though I wasn't an officer or in advanced.

It was just another unusual thing that happened to me.

One of the regrets I have from my college years was that I didn't go to Columbia when I had the opportunity. I met a student while at Illinois who was from Columbia. He was trying to learn English, and I was taking a Spanish class. I walked past his residence hall every day to go to class. I don't know how we started talking, but one time he came out of his dormitory and we walked together. Somehow, we came to the agreement that we would meet, and he would only speak in English and I would only speak in Spanish. We didn't hang-out together other than our sessions of learning each other's language, and walking together each day, but we ended up becoming good friends.

Summer came and he invited me down to Columbia. His father was an architect in Bogotá, the capital of Columbia. Their family owned a summer house on the ocean in Cartagena. He even had his own monkey there! He told me that I wouldn't have to pay for a thing except for my way there. What an opportunity that would have been.

I told him "no," that I had to go wash cars at the dealership for the summer. I always regretted that I didn't take the opportunity to visit my friend when I had it.

This evidently made a lasting impression on me. Currently my Donna and I are both looking at a tour that goes to these two cities.

The summer of my Junior year in college, Donna and I went to her parents' house in Westtown PA., just outside of Philadelphia. We told them that we would like to get married. We were having dinner when I brought it up, and her father, who had just taken a ladle of soup, spit it out. He composed himself and asked a question that I thought I could answer: "How are you proposing you will support my daughter in a manner she has been accustomed to?"

I had it all figured out. I told her parents that we planned on using the money that she receives from them, and the money that I received from my parents, and together, we would use those funds to financially make it.

It sounded good at the time.

I was quickly informed that I better rethink my plan. Donna's father told me that when she leaves the family to be married, she won't be receiving any more money. For college, bills, or anything.

We decided to wait until after she graduated and got a job teaching before we would marry. Donna graduated with a degree in Speech Correction and had a contract to teach in Decatur, Illinois.

It took me longer to graduate. I transferred from Illinois to Millikin University in Decatur. I say that I "transferred" because it sounds a whole lot better than saying I flunked out.

After two years at Illinois, I switched majors. I found myself needing some prerequisites in the School of Business that I had not taken in the School of Liberal Arts. My solution was to go to summer school and take the accounting and economics classes that I needed.

This plan sounded like it would work. The fraternity house was not open in the summer, so I had to rent a room at a rooming house. I also got a job at the campus beer garden which paid my bills and furnished my meals. At work, I would see some of my past instructors drinking beer. I would join them after I got off work. This cut into the time that I should have spent studying.

My roommate that summer was a retired officer from the Air Force. He would take me to the local air base to party. This also didn't help my cause to get in the prerequisites I needed that summer.

That summer, I had a great time, socially. But academically, my study habits were poor, and I flunked both classes. That put me on scholastic probation. When the next semester at Illinois rolled around, my grades were not high enough to pull my overall grade point average above the minimum requirement to stay in school. I realize that my lack of studying, my focus on Donna, and practice every night on the fencing team did not help my situation. Before summer school, I didn't seem to have a problem with my grades, but losing a grip on whatever grade point I had going into that summer semester didn't hold and I just couldn't recover.

I picked Millikin University because of its close proximity to Champaign. I could easily stay at my Fraternity house and visit Donna in Champaign on the weekends, then return to Decatur for classes during the week.

While at Milliken, I vowed to myself that I would make my grades a priority. I knew I was smarter than a lot of other people, but I never really learned how to study. I decided I would teach myself to study and get good grades by going to the University at night and study in a sound-proof music practice room. I would sit there in the quiet and memorize all of my lessons. This worked for me, my instructors liked me, and I ended up graduating on the Dean's List. I'm proud of this acknowledgement. It took a lot of work for me to receive it.

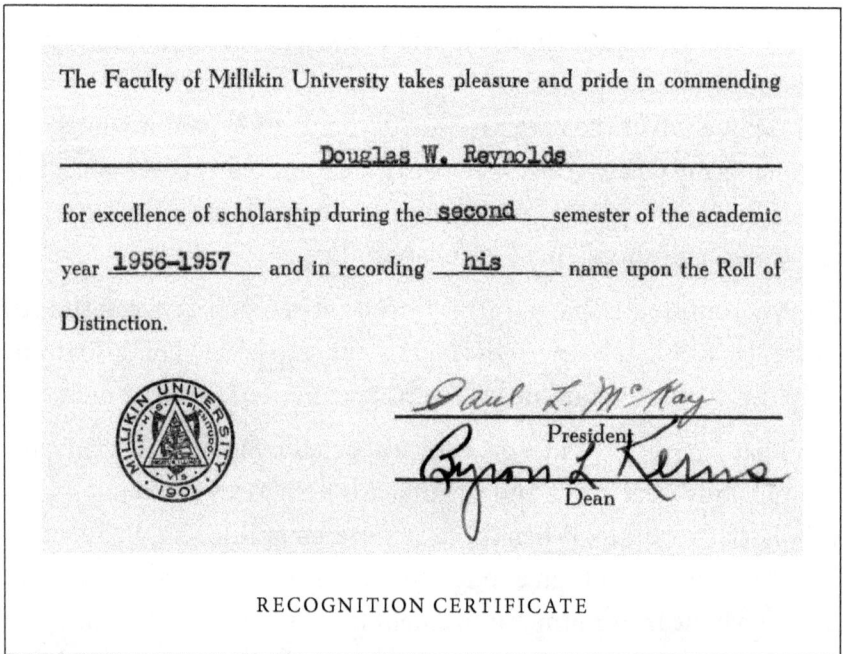

The Faculty of Millikin University takes pleasure and pride in commending

Douglas W. Reynolds

for excellence of scholarship during the **second** semester of the academic year **1956-1957** and in recording **his** name upon the Roll of Distinction.

Paul L. McKay
President

Byron L. Kerns
Dean

RECOGNITION CERTIFICATE

The summer after Donna graduated, we were married and moved to Decatur where she taught, and I finished my classes to graduate with a high recognition. I hold on to this recognition to show that I wasn't really dumb for flunking out; I just didn't know how to study well.

That is another regret that I have—that I didn't learn how to really study sooner.

DONNA AND DOUG

College Memories

Joined Sigma Pi Fraternity

Military Ball Dance Program

R.O.T.C Captain and West Point Recommendation

Quarter-finalist—All University in Badminton

Practiced with the Freshman Tennis Team

Tested for proficiency out of Tennis Class

University of Illinois Fencing Team

Invitation to Bogota, Columbia

Summer School Job at Kam's (Beer Joint)

Worked at a Soda Fountain at. Milliken—Robbery

Job Interview—Plumbing Valves

First home with Donna—a trailer. Sale was risky.

CHAPTER FOUR

Reynolds Motor Company; DBA Reynold's Ford

THE FIRST HOME Donna and I lived in after we married was a trailer. When we decided to sell the trailer, I was kind of trusting and dumb. The guy wrote us a check and left. Thankfully the check was good.

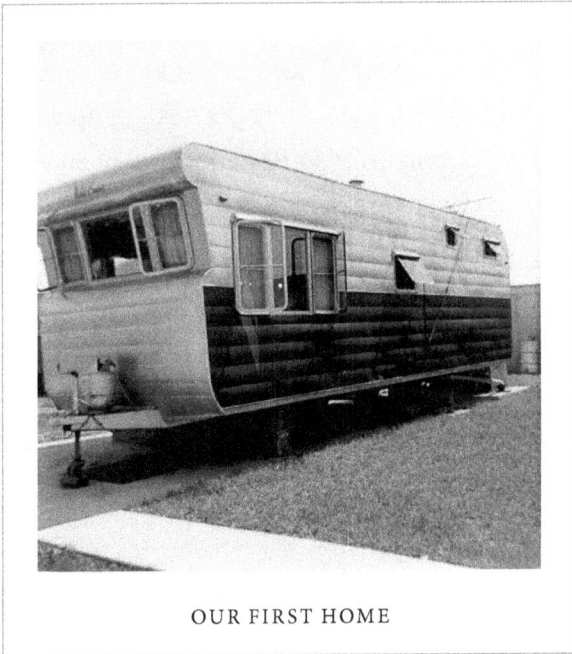

OUR FIRST HOME

We moved from Decatur back to where I grew up and I started selling cars in the family business. Donna was pregnant at the time. We borrowed some money from my mom for a down payment on a house that was relatively new. The builder was the only one who had lived in it. Getting back into the dealership business started to feel like we were living the good life. I made $400 a month and we had around $20 left to spend after our mortgage was paid and other expenses. It's funny now that I look back on that time and think it truly did feel like "the good life."

I started back to work at the dealership in the spring of '57. After my dad passed away, my mom was able to become a dealer for the business. Obviously, when I was in college, I was unable to take on this role. When I returned to the family business, I had to prove myself before I could step into the dealer position. The used car manager at that time could see the writing on the wall. He knew that I would eventually be taking over the business, so he left and opened up his own used car lot.

The general sales manager, Dale Lindquist, was under the impression that he would someday take over the dealership. When he didn't, Ford gave him the opportunity in Bettendorf to open up a dealership where there hadn't been one before. In the fall of '59, he left to open his dealership and he took a number of my employees with him including my office manager. There I was, just a young kid in the business, without a lot of knowledge on how to run the place. What I lacked in knowledge, I made up for in desire.

It seemed that everyone tried to take advantage of me. Many did. I had a lot to learn. My whole focus was to improve, grow and survive. It worked.

Our family grew and so did the business. My work schedule was seven days and six nights a week. We were only supposed to be open from 10-2 on Sundays, but if there was a customer there, I was there. The only time I had with family or to cut grass or do anything other than work at the dealership was on Sunday afternoons. It took a while before we decided to cut back to two nights and six days a week, but eventually we backed off. It was just too brutal on the family, on me, and indirectly, on our customers. When I was working seven days a week, by the time Monday rolled around and it was time to unlock the doors, my attitude towards customers was like "What the hell do you want?" Of course, I never did or said that, but the burnout was there.

When I first got back and started working, there were two identical buildings and a one-car showroom with a clean-up department in the back. One building was on the north side of the street, one on the south side. My dad only owned the building on the north side and had to eventually vacate the building on the south side. I think the owner of the other building wanted more rent or something. In 1958, Ford was pushing to have more modern facilities, which meant we were going to need to construct a new showroom next to the existing building on the north side. There was an empty lot that belonged to the dealership, so that was no problem. A small tavern and a house on the corner were purchased and torn down. There is a picture in 1958 showing cars all lined up on the gravel from the building to the corner. At that time, I stood there and said, "This is all the room we will ever need!"

We built a three-car showroom and had cars parked from the building to the corner. It was modern and seemed like a lot. I remember an old-timer salesman who had worked for my dad came out on the lot one day and said, "Hey kid, you made a big mistake. You should have gone up on the hill." I thought he was a dumb, old man who didn't know what he was talking about. I knew for certain that I had all I would ever need.

A couple years later, I was parking cars in two remote sites because business had increased and so had my inventory. I guess that old salesman wasn't a dumb, old man after all.

Ford continued to push for more modern facilities. I went to the neighbor on the east side of our lot. He had an empty lot and a house.

I asked if I could buy his land. His sister lived in the small house so I told him she could still live there until she passed away. Then I would tear it down to add on to the dealership. He gave me a price that was extremely high. He owned the rest of that block, so I guess he thought he had me trapped and I would pay the high price. I kept looking at other options.

I found a piece of land up on the hill that I thought was just beautiful. You had to veer either a little to the right or a little to the left in order to go by it. I imagined how great it would be to put a big Ford sign out there where everyone who went by would see it. It was the perfect place.

EXPANDED THE OLD FACILITIES

I met with the owner and we walked the property. I asked him how much he wanted per acre. He gave me a price that I thought was fair and I told him I'd take five acres. But the owner said he would only sell it if I bought all forty acres. I couldn't afford forty. My whole posture fell when he said that.

He mentioned to me that he had another property for sale, so we went there. It was just a field that was kind of elevated. I stood up on the hill and looked at the cars going by. I thought it wasn't too bad either. I said I would take five acres, and again, the landowner said I would have to buy the entire thirteen acres. I couldn't afford that either. Today, this property is where Green Chevrolet is located.

He showed me one more area that only had three acres. Ford had told me that I needed at least three acres, but I knew I needed five. The guy selling the land said, "Well I don't know what to tell ya' then." He got in his car and drove back to Muscatine where he lived.

NEW FACILITY ON THE HILL

I was left standing there, feeling dejected. I happened to look up across the street at a little farmhouse with a small barn. I got in my car, drove over there and knocked on the door. A little, old lady in bedroom slippers shuffled to the door and I asked her if she would be interested in selling her land. "Sonny," she said, "you're a day too late. I just sold it."

PRESENT FACILITY

Of course she did. But then she went on to tell me that she didn't know if the people who bought it really wanted it. Really? I learned that she sold her property to the Rock Island County Fair Board. I knew the president of the board, he worked for the City of East Moline and I had sold vehicles to the city. I contacted him and, long story short, they wanted the land so they could access the back of their property. They didn't really need all the land but didn't know what else to do. They were tickled that I was interested in it.

I bought five frontage acres there and gave them a sixty-foot right of way to get back to their land. That would give them two access points from 13th Street and from 42nd Avenue, which is now Avenue of the Cities. A year or two later, I bought two more acres from them.

We were there for three or four years when a guy who owned the frontage land next to us said he would sell it to me. This was in 1979 when the interest rates were 20%. I thought the price was too high compared to the other property I purchased, so I turned him down. I later saw some people out there measuring and learned they were planning on buying the property to build a furniture store. I didn't want them to build it up close to the road and block the view to my dealership. As it turned out, they backed out of buying the land. I ended up going to the bank and borrowed money at 20% to buy this frontage. I wanted the protection of knowing that the view of the dealership would not be obstructed.

Finally, land on the back side of that property became available. I didn't really want it, but they ended up giving me a good deal, so I bought it. Now that is our whole package of acreage that Reynolds Ford has. It is what we have to this day.

Somewhere around 2003, I built the new body shop and remodeled all of the offices and showroom. It is now 2019 and that is the current status of the land and buildings of Reynolds Motor Company; DBA Reynold's Ford.

Reynolds Ford Memories

Sold first Ranchero in Chicago District after
two years managing dealership

Finalist for Illinois small business awards

The meeting when it was announced that
Bunkie Knudsen was fired

1982, won national sales contest and a trip to Europe

Sponsored tennis tournament for muscular dystrophy

Played tennis with President of Ford Motor Credit Co.

Sold the first contour model in the Chicago District

CHAPTER FIVE

Our Journey to Success

A S THE PROGRESSION and success of the business grew, we were able to sell more cars and make more money. Personally, I didn't have any money as I put it all back into the growing business; I had to borrow everything in order to grow and build the business. As business increased, we were paying off debt so we could have a better place, have more inventory, sell more cars, and earn more customers.

While I was growing a successful business, I ended up receiving a lot of awards. Two of the most notable were the National Ford Dealers Council Award and the Time Magazine Quality Dealer Award.

The Dealer Council Award was through Ford. Local districts that make up regions across the United States and are represented by Ford dealers. Our region included Chicago, Milwaukee, Minneapolis, St. Louis, and the Davenport Districts. I had gone to local dealer council meetings and participated. It's really kind of a wild thing where everybody vents their problems with Ford Motor Company. These issues are codified down to some recommendations that then go to the regional meetings. The regional representatives eventually go on to the Nationals. After going to and participating in several district and regional meetings, our local district manager, a gentleman by the name of Joe Collier, suggested I run for the National Dealer Council. At the time, I really didn't know why he would suggest such a thing or why he thought I would be capable. He continued to encourage me.

In retrospect, I recognize that Joe was a man of faith whom I now believe God sent to me to show me that I could do something bigger than I thought I could. I needed that.

I ran for and was awarded that national position. There were only twenty-two others that represented the regions across the country, so this was a big honor. During the National meeting, we were in Detroit for a week and went through all the recommendations from the dealers all over the U.S. and codified it down to twelve different actions that we could take to Henry Ford II and his brother, William Clay Ford. Also present at the meeting were the heads of each division within Ford Motor Company.

The meeting was held at the Central Staff office building. The boardroom was a large, dramatic room with deep red carpet. The table that made up the desks were lit with can lights from above so the light would hit your table just right. There was a little drawer, paper and pencil, and your name in front of each of the regional representatives from around the country.

All of the sudden, while we were seated in this room, a door that you can't see located in a wall opens up and in walks Henry Ford II and William Clay Ford, followed by the department heads.

For the next hour or so, we talked about the recommendations that were submitted ahead of time for them to see what they could provide by way of answers. After the meeting, we went up to the executive dining room which was on or near the top of the multiple-story building. You could see daffodils blooming on a ledge that went all around the outside of the glass walls. They called this the "glass house." Back in its day, it was one of the early, all-glass buildings. The daffodils were in full bloom, the waiters were in all white coats with black ties. This was a huge contrast to the Deere & Co. executive dining room, which was on a lower floor of the building looking out on the "swan pond," and the waitresses in nondescript, uniform dresses.

The other big award was the Time Quality Dealer Award. Time Magazine had an award for the best-quality, all-makes automotive dealer in the United States. In order to be considered, you had to send in a resumé and be sponsored by the state you are located in. I was the dealer sponsored by Illinois. The judging was extensive. I had to send photos and information about services and customer relations. This wasn't just about sales, either. Involvement in the community was a very big factor.

The judging took place in multiple stages, cutting nominees down to eighteen finalists. This was for all car dealers, not just Ford. I was one of the finalists.

The awards ceremony was held at the Las Vegas Convention Center during the National Automobile Dealer's Annual Convention. I always tell people that there were 25,000 people in attendance waiting to find out who the dealer was to win the top award. I didn't win it, but being a finalist was honor enough. The rest of that story is that those 25,000 people were actually there to hear Lee Iacocca, who happened to be speaking immediately following the awards ceremony.

All finalists for this award had a life-size picture at the entrance of the exhibition hall. Each of us then had a full-page photo featured in Time Magazine, along with information about how we were elected. It's neat to be able to hold a magazine with your picture on it and say that you were featured in Time Magazine. I still have copies of it.

Besides these two big awards, I was very active in the community. There are numerous articles written in newspapers and business magazines concerning my work and volunteer efforts.

TIME MAGAZINE
QUALITY DEALER AWARD
FINALIST

DOUGLAS W. REYNOLDS

Douglas W. Reynolds, president, Reynolds Motor Company, East Moline, Illinois.

TIME Magazine, together with the National Automobile Dealers Association, recently honored distinguished automobile dealers as the recipients of the eighteenth annual TIME Magazine Quality Dealer Award.

One of the finalists is Douglas W. Reynolds, from E. Moline, Illinois. He is among those chosen for their outstanding performance, both as good automobile dealers and as valued citizens of their communities.

TIME is proud to give these outstanding people the recognition they've earned.

1987

TIME MAGAZINE FEATURE

I started a foundation for the City of East Moline. It is similar to The Great River Bend Foundation and its purpose is to give money away to good causes. Moline also has a foundation and I approached the head of that to find out how I could start one for East Moline. After a few months of trying to figure out how to get a foundation started, I ended up calling a few people together and inviting the Rock Island Foundation and Moline Foundation to give us a presentation on how they first began. We found out it would take a minimum of two million dollars and file specific tax forms in order to create a new foundation. We ended up becoming an independent affiliate of the Moline Foundation.

Moline also had a group called "Renew Moline." It is made up of businesspeople who want to work with the city in order to contribute and do things that the city itself cannot. For example, in order to take hazardous property, the city is required to go through a lengthy process of hoops and paperwork. Private citizens are able to buy old buildings and rehab them. I wanted to start something similar in East Moline. We named it "REDEEM—Revitalize and Develop East Moline." This organization is still going today.

I was the first president of the newly created citizen's advisory council. This was an effort to try and improve the city, so the Mayor and Economic Development people came to me and we put together a group of people to brainstorm what this should look like. REDEEM was actually born out of the efforts of this group.

One of the first major projects to go through REDEEM was this master plan to enhance and build up an area in East Moline. A restaurant was on board to build and we had an unofficial go-ahead to plan for an office building, as well as condos on the water. Two major things happened that hindered this development. The first was that the city did not want to spend money for a road to get to the proposed development, and two, the developer said there was no way to move forward without a road. We still were able to get two big condos and four smaller ones built. The rest of the plans are still in place but have not yet come to fruition.

Another sponsorship I am proud to be able to do is a rotary scholarship for graduating seniors. The Rotary club has a program called Strive. Originally, the program would identify and take underperforming students in high school and give them an opportunity to enter into a competition for a chance to win free tuition at Black Hawk College for two years. The school identifies the students, and those who participate attend a rotary meeting with their parents and the committee chair will talk about how their GPA has improved. It's a really good program, but none of the kids would end up going on beyond the two years at Black Hawk, if they even decided to go to Black Hawk. I wanted to identify people who had the scholarship ability to attend college but could not afford it. Now, the high school picks a person every year that falls into that category, I personally pay their tuition at Black Hawk and their tuition at Western if they transfer after two years. With one new student each year, the pipeline is full when I have two students at Black Hawk and two students at Western. It comes to about $16,000 per year.

I am glad that these students have the drive and intellectual ability, and now, the money, to go on to graduate with a four-year degree. I don't do this for recognition. I'm just glad that I can contribute to further the education of a deserving student who wouldn't be able to afford it otherwise. I hope to continue offering this to deserving students.

As you can see, I'm proud of the work I've done and the things I've accomplished. It's only as I look back in hindsight when I recognize that the awards, gifts, and recognition I've received are not of my own doing at all. God provided the opportunities and the means for me to participate in work I enjoy and the rewards I've been given. Before I found faith, I thought it was all because of me. Now I know better.

Doug Reynolds, left, of Reynolds Motor Co., retiring president of Revitalize and Develop East Moline (REDEEM), and John Gault, general manager of John Deere Harvester Works, receive keys to the city from Mayor Bill Ward during Monday evening's East Moline City Council meeting. It was Mr. Ward's last meeting as mayor.

Doug Reynolds is East Moline Citizen of Year

By Katie Schallert
Staff writer

EAST MOLINE — What do the chief of police, a car salesman and a Rotarian have in common?

All will be honored by the East Moline Citizen Advisory Committee and the Rotary Club of East Moline Oct. 25 for their service to the city.

The city's Citizen of the Year Doug Reynolds is president of Reynolds Motor Co., 1900 42nd Ave., East Moline. He has been active in such activities as the Rotary Club, Quad City Riverfront Council, Revitalize and Redevelop East Moline, Black Hawk College Board and the library board. He is a past president of the Illinois Quad Cities Chamber of Commerce

According to his nomination, Mr. Reynolds was raised in the Quad-Cities area and graduated from United Township High School. He received a bachelor of science degree from Millikin University and has worked full time at Reynolds Motor Co. since 1957.

■ Winner of the Denny Jacobs Public Service Award is Police Chief Gary Sutton. His nomination said, "He is a shining example of a person dedicated to the betterment of our community in both his personal and professional life.

The Denny Jacobs award recognizes "Someone who shows outstanding support

Doug Reynolds

Gary Sutton

for the community," according to the application.

■ Earnest Reischmann of Cordova garnered the Rotarian of the Year Award. He owned Ernie's Auto Service in Silvis.

Earnest Reischmann

He serves on the Rotary Board of Directors and has had a perfect attendence record since recovering from a stroke a few years ago.

The three men will be honored at the Short Hills Country Club in East Moline. Tickets are $20 a person. The evening starts with a reception at 6:30 p.m., followed by dinner at 7, a choral presentation from United Township High School at 8 and the awards presentation at 8:30.

Those wishing to attend should call 752-1589 to make reservations.

Reynolds unveils expansion

By Rita Pearson
Staff writer

Reynolds Motor Co. founder E.J. Reynolds sold cars so finance his chiropractic studies at Palmer College.

Some of these former customers remit getting adjustments from the auto dealer, proclaims Brent Reynolds, vice president and general sales manager and remedy.

The East Moline Ford dealership celebrated an adjustment of a different kind Thursday, as it unveiled a multimillion dollar expansion and remodeling project.

"The city of East Moline is very proud of what you've done," Mayor Bill Ward said during brief ribbon-cutting ceremonies marking the dealership's $5,000 square-foot expansion. "Your dad would be very proud. I know your mother is. I talked with her inside before the ceremony. I always say the best dealership east of the Mississippi River is right here in East Moline."

Doug Reynolds, owner of Reynolds Motor Company in East Moline, shakes the hand of Ross Roberts, Ford Motor Co. vice president and general manager of Ford Division, after cutting the ribbon opening the new multi-million dollar expansion and remodeling project.

Ross Roberts, Ford vice president and general manager of the Ford Division, commended the family-owned dealership for its longevity and commitment to the community.

"The average life of an auto dealership in America is eight years," Mr. Roberts said. "For you to have gone 66 years is truly phenomenal."

Mr. Roberts and owner Doug Reynolds cut the ceremonial red ribbon in the ceremony, which marked the first of a three-day celebration. Other Ford executives and the Illinois Quad City Chamber of Commerce ambassadors also participated in the ceremony.

The dealership remodeled the showroom and entrance and added new offices, handicapped accessible rest rooms and a customer lounge during the past year. A separate 12,000-square-foot state-of-the-art auto and body shop opened last fall to the west of the showroom and service center. The body shop can accommodate up to 26 vehicles at a time.

Founded in 1935, Reynolds Motor Co. is celebrating 66 years

of incorporation with special sales promotions. The company has 106 employees.

Jobs & Money

Doug Reynolds a passionate advocate of the Mississippi River

By Jonathan Turner
Staff writer

EAST MOLINE — More than 40 years after taking over Reynolds Ford from his father in 1966, Doug Reynolds is semi-retired. But that doesn't mean he isn't busy.

The head of the former Moline and East Moline chambers of commerce and East Moline Rotary, the silver-haired auto magnate keeps community wheels turning as president of Revitalize and Develop East Moline (REDEEM) and River Action. Mr. Reynolds — a passionate advocate of the Mississippi River — also is a dealer for Hunter sailboats.

"REDEEM is like a full-time job," he said, noting day-to-day operation of the Ford dealership has been in the hands of son, Scott, for 18 months. The elder Reynolds gives his time because of his affection for the area.

"I feel that it's provided a good home to raise a family, provided a good living," he said.

Business leader

"He's a very good leader, one of the most optimistic people I've worked with," said Metrobank president Gary Andersen, a REDEEM board member. "He always tries to find a way to make things work. He's a tireless worker for REDEEM.

"He's tenacious. If he believes in a project, he's going to stick with it."

River Action executive director Kathy Wine credited Mr. Reynolds with the idea to redefine the river to help the Quad-Cities rebound in the early '90s.

"He's definitely a visionary," she said. "He's good at articulating that and selling it. He's also good at the details, to see that needs had to be met with funding. He's been an inspiration for me. I've never seen anyone who's as forward-thinking and hard-working."

Like many others, Mr. Reynolds grew up taking the

Doug Reynolds

Age: 67
Title: President, Reynolds Motor Co.
Education: Bachelor's in business from Millikin University.
Family: Wife, Donna; children Sherri, 43, Scott, 40, and grandchildren Suni, 17, Billy, 15, Carolyn, 12, Alexandra, 5, Jonathan and Jackson, both 2.

river for granted. That changed in 1970, when he fell in love with sailing during a trip to Florida. In 1982, he championed the idea of the river as a natural asset, which led to a year of activities and formation of River Action in 1985 to revitalize the area's entire riverfront.

Whether it's bringing more people to see the beauty and recreational advantages of the Missis-

sippi River, or redeveloping abandoned or blighted parts of East Moline, Mr. Reynolds wants to improve the community's image.

"It's having projects that will put another jewel in the crown of the Quad-Cities," he said. "We feel our sports center, office building, condos, interpretive center, train station and water taxi will do that."

Reynolds Ford — the area's top-selling Ford dealer — was founded in 1925 by Erdie Reynolds as a Horst-Strieter dealership. Doug Reynolds worked for his dad part-time since 4th grade, and full-time after his death.

Since 1975, Scott Reynolds has worked for his dad, from washing cars to being vice president, which is a joy for the proud papa.

"He's a natural for it," the older Mr. Reynolds said. "He's going to be better than I was. You can see it."

Staff writer Jonathan Turner can be reached at 786-6441, Ext. 251, or by e-mail at jonathan@qconline.com.

Doug Reynolds of Reynolds Ford, in East Moline, a business leader and REDEEM president, who's also active with River Action and other boards.

Memories and headlines showcasing the journey to success

CHAPTER SIX

Glitz, Glory, and a Carefree Life

I N THE 1950S AND 60S, it was difficult to get together at Christmas time with Donna's parents. They would take the train and it would freeze up. Prop planes at that time were undependable as far as the weather goes. In 1969, we decided to meet in Naples, Florida for a family Christmas gathering.

When we were there, I immediately became enamored with the place. I was looking around and found a new development that I wanted to show my father-in-law, and later the women. I found a three-bedroom, three-bathroom townhouse on the water with a dock for $50,000. We bought it jointly, each paying $25,000. I borrowed my half. Somewhere around 2009, I learned it was on the market for a million dollars!

There were eight townhouses in a row, a pool, and an eighteen-unit apartment building. In an adjacent harbor area, people owned rather large boats. I couldn't afford a large boat and I was wondering what I would do with the dock and water area we now owned. I saw a catamaran coming in, and that's when I knew what I would do—I'd buy a sailboat.

I took the kids downtown with me to purchase a sailboat. That was the beginning of a long love I have had for the recreation and sport of sailing.

I became completely captivated when sailing. It gave me a sense of peace that I could not obtain any other way. There is something magical about being out on the water and propelling a boat with just you and the Lord.

Year after year, my love for sailing increased. I bought a very small sailboat at first and taught myself to sail. Later, I had some friends who recommended I join a sailing club. We raced sailboats at this club.

RACING SAILBOATS

With that, I wanted to do more with sailing. I quit playing summer tennis, bought a sailboat, and joined the local sailing club. When I wanted to sail even more than that, I bought a house on the river in Port Byron so I could sail every day. We lived in that house from Memorial Day to Labor Day every year for 25 years. It was local so I could still work every day and sail when I came home. I sold it after my wife became ill and we could no longer go there.

SUMMER HOUSE ON THE MISSISSIPPI

During that time, I became a better sailor and I wanted to sail even bigger boats. I've heard this about people who sail—you always want a bigger boat. I took sailing lessons for a bigger boat through classes taught on Captiva Island in Florida. When the training was complete, I met three other fellows who had the same instructor at a different time that I had, and after graduating from these courses, we were placed together through the school to go sailing and put to use the knowledge we gained. We met in St. Martin and sailed together where we got along fine. The next year, I contacted the three other men and asked if they wanted to charter a boat ourselves. We did and sailed the British Virgin Islands. One fellow was a foot doctor from Florida, one was a German who lives in Mexico, and the third fellow was an entrepreneur from Dallas. I still can't tell you what he does, but he bought a three-million-dollar lot in Naples and is building a house on it. Whatever he does, he is doing well.

That set the course for the next fifteen years. Each year, we would jointly decide where to go, charter a boat, and we took turns, rotating who would make arrangements, to be the skipper of record, etc. We went to some pretty exotic places in those fifteen years. Almost everywhere in the Caribbean from Antigua to Tobago Cays, and from St. Lucia down. We also picked a boat up in Miami and sailed it to Key West. On that trip, we partied all night and sailed all day. We went to Upper Belize and Lower Belize, as well as Abaco Islands and the British Virgin Islands. We went to Baha where there was unbelievably amazing wildlife.

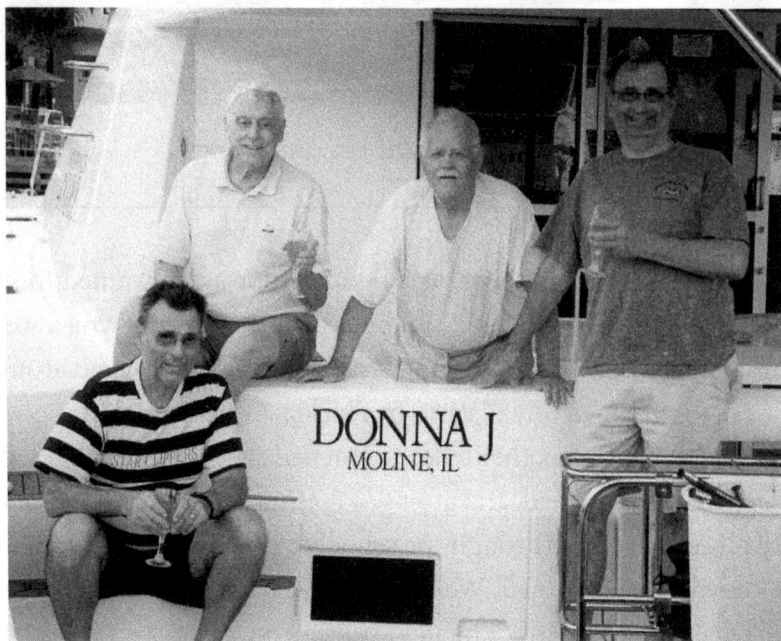

SAILING TOGETHER FOR FIFTEEN YEARS

We went to Rio where we visited the Statue of Christ. We hired a cab that day and were driving from the Statue of Christ back down to the beach. Over ahead were these hang-gliding. When we got to the beach a fellow had come over and asked us if we wanted to go hang-gliding. I didn't want to because I didn't like heights. This guy said hang-gliding was just like sailing, with just the wind and the quiet and no motor. The others in our group looked at me and asked if I was going. I said "yep." I figured if I was ever going to do it, I better do it now.

My friend and I hopped in the back of a pick-up truck and started up the mountain. At the top there was a plateau. I was asked if I could run, and of course I could. The guy locks arms with me and says, "When I say go, run with me." So, I take off and run really fast with him. We turned around and did it again. I was then instructed to put on a helmet and he walked me over to the edge of a cliff. I had to put a harness on, and there was a strange wing contraption laying on the ground. I figured what was going to happen was that I would have to run and somehow the wing contraption laying on the ground behind me would have to get above me, I just didn't understand how.

When I'm all strapped in, the guy does some strange chanting. "Wait a minute!" I shouted. "How is this thing supposed to get above me?"

"It will happen," the guy says and then goes back into his chanting. I hesitated. But I knew if I didn't do it now, I never would. After the third chant, we took off.

He gave me two rules for hang-gliding: not to look down and not to touch him. The wings went above us, and I look down and grab him. He yelled at me, "Let go of me or we'll crash!" He told me to look at the wing. There was a camera there. I have some pictures.

Everything from then on was fine. I didn't look down and it was quite pretty. When it was time to land, the guy doesn't do it with a nice glide-landing on the beach, but rather a zoom-like landing on the grass. I thought he was dropping way too fast.

It was over and he asked me how I liked it. I told him it was terrible. He bought me a beer and the problem was solved.

I later found out that this guy was hurrying to dump me because there was a movie star that wanted to go hang-gliding and he wanted to be the one to take her. I guess I could forgive him for that!

On one of our sailing trips, we flew to Salvador. Back then, if you took a sailboat with no motor and wanted to come across from Europe, you'd take the Tradewinds and end up in Salvador, Brazil. It was easy sailing and a good time. On this trip, we raced a handmade workboat that was coming along with storage and cargo in it. The people manning the boat knew sailing. We ended up side-by-side and were going to turn in the same direction. Any time two sailboats get together, it ends up being a race. So, I was on the helm and I knew if I got on the windward side of the workboat, I would block the wind from their sails. We shot past them. The guy on the other boat wanted to race the next day, but we weren't planning on staying.

One of our last sailing trips together was magical Tahiti. The waters were unbelievably clear. This trip was probably the crown jewel of the climate for sailing. Every place we ever sailed had its own challenge. We were given a map of the ocean and we had to figure out how to get from point A to point B. The people would tell us what hazards to avoid, but the rest was up to us.

Sailing was just a thrill of the wind, making the boat go, not getting into any trouble, and being able to stop and see all the new sights. We were exposed to different cultures and people. It was like a "Jimmy Buffet" time. Everything was sunshine, cocktails, and fair winds. We did get bigger boats as we went along throughout the fifteen years we sailed together. There was always something exciting and different than what we had done before. Every port and every year we experienced a different set of circumstances. It was one of the most thrilling times of my life.

After my wife became ill, I quit sailing. Years later, I decided that I wanted to experience the thrill and joy that I once had when I sailed. I went sailing with the German one time and was on my way home when I looked through a sailing magazine. There was an ad for sailboat. The guy on the plane in the seat next to me asked if I was going to buy one. I told him I was thinking about it. He said if I decide to do it, I should go to The Moorings. They are the largest sailboat charter company in the world.

I bought a "crewed" sailboat from The Moorings. The crew actually lived on the boat and protected it. We had a captain and a cook. When I'm not on the boat, they charter it out and keep that revenue, and they paid me money as a part of a five-year program. At the end of these five years, you can take the boat yourself, sell it, or re-up with the company with a new boat. At my age, I just couldn't see re-upping and ending up in my 90's with a sailboat to sell. I just put it up with a broker this year (2019).

THE DONNA J

Sailing represents a carefree time in my life. Everything was unusual and like Jimmy Buffet's "Margaritaville." No shoes, no shirt, no problem. It's hard to fully express what I mean. The fresh air is different. The sun and the breeze, everything about it is just beautiful.

At the time, I didn't look at sailing as something from God, but in retrospect, I can see how it was God's wind, God's sun, and God's blue water. There was a closeness I felt to God's world in a way that I never had on hard pavement and in cars.

Another thing that happened after I joined the local sailing club was that I started selling boats. I became a dealer and had a demonstrator boat from the company that I would sail on the Mississippi River. This was a smaller racing sailboat that one person could handle. I had people tell me that they didn't want a racing sailboat, they wanted one for pleasure. The manufacturer didn't have many dealers, so I gave up this franchise and finally ended up with a line of sailboats that I had done some business with at the Chicago Sailboat Show. This was huge. Every year, I would get a bigger one of their boats to the point of having a 26-foot sailboat that would sleep four people and had a little galley in the head of it. This is what kind of primed me to learn how to sail bigger boats again. I had given up on this business of selling boats when I sold the river house because I was not able to demonstrate them.

But it is kind of neat to say that I sold a boat to the president of Allied Insurance. After he retired from Allied, he was the CEO of Casey's General Store. He bought the boat and had it shipped to his home in Kawi, Hawaii.

In the early '90s, I had the opportunity to play tennis against the Illinois Governor Jim Edgar. Incidentally, he was the last governor in Illinois to have a balanced budget. There was a fundraiser taking place at the Kewanee Country Club. A gal who worked for the republican party and played tennis at the club with my daughter contacted me to see if I wanted to play. I thought she meant that they were going to play doubles and needed a partner for that. I agreed and later found out it was going to be just me playing against the governor.

We met beforehand and walked up the courts to warm up. I thought he wasn't a bad tennis player, but he wasn't that great either. I beat him. Afterwards, we went back down to the locker rooms for a shower before the banquet. This was around the same time I was on the State of Illinois Dealer's Executive Committee. I don't remember what the cause was, but we were trying to pass some legislation. I brought it up with the governor, but he didn't want to be bothered with it. This was just a tennis match.

That's okay. Who else can say they've played tennis and showered with the governor?

Tennis was a big part of my life. At one point, I bought a house in Florida so I could play more tennis. I met a guy there who was a really good player. He played tennis games for money and I enjoyed the challenge of playing with him. I never beat him but before it was time to go back home, I was playing pretty even with him. It was something I looked forward to each time I was there.

I can't say that I ever played tennis just for the enjoyment of the sport. In my younger years, it was a way to fit in. I played for the win and acknowledgement. Later in life, I played for the simple fact that I was better than other people my age. I could play against people who were ten to twenty years younger and still win. I would compete with people in higher status positions than I, and they couldn't beat me. Tennis was more about my ego than anything.

When I was eighty, I had my first encounter with the Senior Olympics. I qualified for nationals in tennis. In the Senior Olympics, when you qualify one year, you compete for the national title the next. Well, in between qualifying and nationals, I tore my rotator cuff, so that was the end of my tennis career.

I still wanted to compete in something, so I took up playing pickleball.

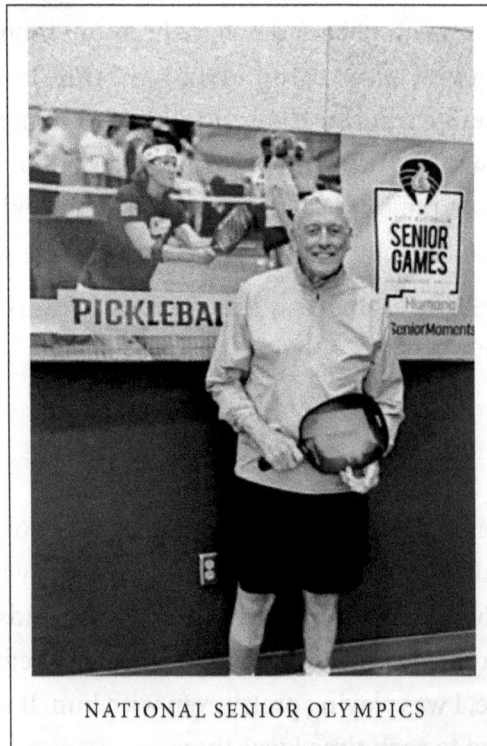

NATIONAL SENIOR OLYMPICS

I ended up competing and winning medals in pickleball. Recently, I went to Albuquerque for the National competition and ended up placing fourth in my age group. It isn't that I started this sport hoping to become the biggest guru of pickleball, but after all of those years of tennis, I just didn't feel good unless I was active. I still wanted to prove that I was as good as or better than others—this is likely what drove me to nationals. But I enjoyed the activity.

I have been exposed to things during my first marriage that I never would have been had it not been for the influence of my job or Donna's family. We stayed in hotels all over the country, flew in airplanes to visit my in-laws, and attended high-class events. It truly was a glamorous lifestyle.

I had a spectacular life. I got the awards, the sales, the sailboats, was club champion in tennis—all the glitz and glam I ever could have hoped for. It seemed I had it all.

But there was one thing I didn't have. The peace that comes from knowing God. I didn't know that was even missing until my first wife passed away and I met my second wife.

Magical, Carefree Memories

Peggy Lee Concert

Shook hands with Doc Severinsen, trumpet player for Johnny Carson

Tennis champion, SouthPark Tennis Club

1970, bought a townhouse in Florida with In-laws

Met Peter Hathaway Capstick, a big game and great white hunter.

Elephant hair bracelet—first seen when meeting Peter Hathaway Capstick

1971, bought a sailboat and taught myself to sail

1973, bought a C-Scow, joined Lake Davenport Sailing Club

1978, sold boat, competed in tennis tournaments

Became a dealer for Melges MC Boat

1983, summer house and sailing

Family Fun Doubles Tournament, won 2nd place in consolation bracket

2001, bought a condo in Florida to play more tennis. Sold in 2005

Played tennis with Governor Jim Edgar and beat him

Sailed for fifteen years with three others

Hang-glided off of 2000-foot mountain in Rio

Sailboat robbed at 5:00 a.m. in Guadalupe

2014, qualified for tennis nationals in singles and doubles

2014, bought the "Donna J.", 2019, put
"Donna J." to broker to sell

2018, Iowa Pickleball, qualified for nationals:
men's singles, men's doubles, and mixed doubles

2019, National. Pickleball Singles, 4th place in 85-year-up category

CHAPTER SEVEN
Troubled Waters

I CAN'T ARGUE THAT I've had a good life, but it wasn't always smooth sailing.

In between the birth of my son and daughter, my wife and I were expecting twins. They were girls and we lost them at birth.

One of the girls was stillborn, and the other had never developed normally. Our family doctor had my wife on a medication that the gynecologist later said she probably shouldn't have been on while pregnant.

This was one of the hardest things we went through, but it was a lot harder on Donna that it was on me. We never saw them when they were born. In those days, mothers had to stay a week in the hospital after every birth. Donna shared a room with another gal and the nurses brought her baby in to see her every day. It was difficult for Donna. Every time that baby was brought in, it only reinforced the reality that she lost her own babies.

The other most difficult time in our lives began with back pain that Donna was having. The orthopedic doctor told us that it might be due to a bad knee that was affecting her back, but that never seemed to be right. We had the knee surgery and still she was in constant pain. It began years ago but grew far worse one year when we were in Florida.

We were invited to another apartment in our Florida complex for a cocktail party. Donna was just not able to stand for any length of time.

We were headed back home (to Illinois) and planned a stop to a place in Northern Florida that did arthroscopic back repairs. That procedure didn't help.

When we returned home, we gave in to the likelihood that Donna would need back surgery, so we visited an orthopedic specialist and Donna went through with the recommended back surgery.

The surgery left her with less back pain. She was sent home with a dry compress and instructions to change it every day. We had those big squares and special medical tape, and I would change the bandage. That was all there was to it.

One day I came home from playing tennis and Donna asked me to change her dressing before I showered. I saw pus coming out from the wound, so I called the doctor. We were sent to Trinity Hospital in Moline. When they saw the severity of the infection, Donna was sent immediately to Trinity in Rock Island where they cut a very large, deep piece out of her lower back because they were afraid the infection would travel up her spinal cord and into the brain.

She had ongoing treatments at the wound doctor on the Iowa side of the river. He tried every treatment he knew of, including stem cells. The wound never did get much better. It took four to five years of trying everything the medical professionals could think of before the wound finally closed.

But the pain never stopped.

By the time we reached our 50th wedding anniversary, Donna was in a wheelchair and able to use a walker on occasion. The walker was mainly for inside, the wheelchair, when we went out for meals and such.

We took a cruise for our 50th anniversary, bringing with us our family. From that time on, things just kept going downhill with Donna's health. She would get up to use her walker and suddenly collapse for seemingly no reason.

It was not long after we returned from this trip that Donna was diagnosed with the same lung disease that her mother had passed away from—Interstitial Pneumonitis. It's a terrible disease that eventually causes you to drown because the lungs fill with fluid instead of air. This is one of those diseases that has a genetic link to it. Donna inherited it.

The diagnosis became a death sentence. The days were a constant stream of going to lung and breathing specialists and participating in an exercise plan intended to lengthen the life span of terminal lung patients. With no cure, things just got worse.

Donna spent more and more time in bed, unable to do many of the normal, daily activities of caring for herself. I learned to do the washing and cooking and whatever else was needed. At first, Donna was able to use a walker, but over time, she would fall more often. I was there to help her get up. The disease had caused her to deteriorate so badly that I had to lift her more and more often. One time, I ended up getting a hernia trying to lift her. I got that fixed and we continued to struggle through together.

The last time she fell at home, it was by the bed. She cut her leg badly, was bleeding, and I was unable to get her up. I called my son to come help me. That was the catalyst which led to the decision to have her stay at the hospital. My son thought it was necessary as well. I could no longer do everything she needed me to do. I guess when you see everything happen every day like I did, you don't realize just how bad things really are.

They worked with her in physical therapy at the hospital, but it was soon apparent that there really wasn't any kind of therapy that could help Donna. The degree of her illness and pain was beyond what the hospital could provide. We had no choice but to move her into a nursing home.

As I look back at this move, I can see that this was exactly what she needed, but I was so close to the situation that it was difficult to recognize that this move was necessary.

I also didn't realize that this would be her last move.

Donna moved into the nursing home in December. I would go see her after I ate breakfast. I came home at noon to make a sandwich and let the dog out. I'd go back to the nursing home until it was time for dinner. I'd make myself a drink, let the dog out, and go back again until visiting hours were over at 9:00 p.m. I'd let the dog out again and then go to sleep. This was my daily routine for about four months.

When Donna was not able to consciously breathe on her own, hospice was called in and took over treatment. They gave her morphine for the pain. From this point until she passed away, things moved pretty quickly. Our daughter, Sherri, and a grandson and granddaughter all came in from out of town rather unexpectedly and for different reasons. But God knew. It was April. Donna passed away right after that. The kids were all able to say goodbye.

We were married for 58 years.

My son's wife, daughter, and granddaughter came over and removed everything that belonged to Donna. All of her clothes and jewelry. Everything was gone. I told everyone I didn't want visitors. I wanted to be alone and they all abided by that.

I have quite a few regrets about how I handled my life while being the primary caretaker for Donna. During this time, I bought a sailboat and ended up getting into a fight with them over financing and down payment issues. I should have never done that. The stress that comes with intense caretaking isn't always apparent and clear and can cause you to not act like you normally would. That was the case for me.

Also during that time, I still went to Rotary meetings. There is one meeting that I cannot get out of my head. It was a normal meeting and people were visiting and joking around. This sounds like an insignificant thing, but I recall telling several dirty jokes this time. It wasn't bad, but completely inappropriate. I know I've said worse things, but for some reason, this particular meeting at this time in my life just sticks out in my mind. Again, stress can make you act in ways you normally wouldn't.

Another regret I have during this season of life—I let Donna die alone. She had asked me not to let her be alone when she died. But on the night she passed away, I went home like I did every other night, having no idea she was close to death. I got the call at six in the morning that she had passed. I felt sick that I broke a promise to her. I honestly didn't know that was the night she would die.

I quit most all of my outside activities while I was caretaking for Donna. I eventually re-joined some of them. But after she passed away, I just didn't want to see anyone. I stayed at the house, watched television, drank, and took care of my dog. I had no idea how my life and process of dealing with grief was going to improve. I don't even know if I considered that.

When you go through deep waters,
I will be with you. When you go through rivers of
difficulty, you will not drown.

Isaiah 43:2 (NLT)

CHAPTER EIGHT

Handing Over the Baton

LONG BEFORE DONNA PASSED, we spent a lot of time talking about what our next steps in life would be. Would our son someday take over the business? Would our daughter be a part of it?

Sherri has two master's degrees and most of her doctorate. It was a long and sometimes hard journey from where she started to where she is now. She was married a couple of times; both ended badly. She has two adult children who have their own successes I like to boast about. One of her master's degrees is in kinesiology, which she has some personal experience with. During her schooling, she had to take some time off for a hip surgery, start back with classes at a two-year school, and then later go on to graduate with her masters.

Sherri teaches at Illinois State and the students there all love her. She wrote a book that the school uses in their curriculum. Sherri volunteers to teach tennis to people with special needs and she and her significant other worked in a field that allowed children with special needs to have access to athletic equipment. I am proud of my daughter and her dedication for all she does. The fact that she did not have an easy road only increases my respect and admiration for her.

When it was time to think about the passing of the baton to the family business, Sherri was already pretty settled in her life. She received her share, which she then sold to her brother, Scott.

When Scott and Sherri were growing up, Scott actually had higher achievement scores than Sherri. When he graduated high school, my wife and I wanted him to go to college. Scott had no intentions of attending college; he wanted to be a jet pilot in the Air Force. When he was rejected because of his eyesight, we insisted that he go to college. We didn't ask, just took him to Illinois State and got him enrolled.

Enrolling him in classes didn't help Scott want to be there at all. He showed us that if he drank beer, smoked marijuana, and didn't show up for classes, they wouldn't keep him. I laugh about it now. It wasn't long after we took him to college that he came home with a dog and started working as the night janitor at the dealership.

The dog would go with him at night and serve as his protection. In the summer, he had to keep all the doors open because it was hot, and he scaled off the grease from the shop floor, hosed it down, and cleaned it all up. It was no small job.

After a while, we found the person that was cleaning the showroom wasn't doing it very well, so we hired a service that would clean the showroom and the shop. Scott then went to work in the body shop, learning everything he needed to know about bodywork and repairs.

Then he went into the parts department and learned that side of the business. After that, he worked in sales and led to working the fleet and lease department, working in finance and insurance, and finally becoming a sales manager and then the general manager. Scott had a rather large exposure to every aspect of the dealership, and he did well in all of them.

I had a general manager because I was gone a lot. With all the work I did in the community, I needed a GM. Some questionable things happened with the general manager that I had, and it became clear that I needed to hire a replacement. When I went to place an ad, Scott was wondering what I was doing and why. "I can do that," he said. "I've been doing most of it when the other guy was here anyway." When he said this, it immediately clicked with me. I knew I had to listen to him and see what he could do. Scott took over as the general manager and he did just fine.

It came time to meet with my CPA who specializes in dealership accounting and discuss succession planning. I needed to have a buy-sell agreement in place, so I worked on this with my CPA. I knew my son wanted to become the dealer. At that time, I had built the body shop, refreshed the facilities and all of the other things with the buildings and land. Unfortunately, there was a mortgage on all of that. I gave half of everything to my daughter, half to my son and was able to do it with zero implication tax-wise for them because the mortgage was about the same as the value of the property. That allowed me to give them everything basically for free. Then Scott bought out Sherri's half, which made sense for both of them.

Looking back, it has been a rewarding experience to watch both my son and daughter progress in their lives and careers. I didn't do everything the right way, I know that. But I worked for something, specifically the business, and it does my heart good to see that I was able to pass that on and watch the next generation of my family move it forward.

Everyone wants to leave behind something of significance. Reynolds Ford Motor Company is a large part of where I found my own significance.

Little did I know that, in the end, nothing matters more than knowing God and having faith. What I wouldn't do to go back and recognize those signs from above and embrace a lifestyle of faith so that I could pass that along.

But you don't know what you don't know.

And I wouldn't find my own faith until I went looking for friendship.

Memories

Ford in the family

Reynolds' third generation marks 75 years in business

By Rita Pearson
rpearson@qconline.com

EAST MOLINE — If your name was Reynolds, growing up as the son of a Ford dealer meant you started at the bottom: sweeping floors and washing cars.

That's how father-son team Doug Reynolds and Scott Reynolds both started in the family business at Reynolds Motor Co. before they graduated into auto parts and used-car sales positions.

The Reynolds Co. was honored recently for 75 years in business and a rare third-generation ownership. The company's history reflects the growth of Ford auto manufacturing and the American auto industry.

Doug Reynolds' father, Erdie O. Reynolds, started Reynolds Motor Co. in 1930 after operating the East Moline dealership as a branch of Horst-Strieter Motors for five years. Car sales were a way to support his education while he was studying to become a chiropractor. He later earned his chiropractic license, and used his practice to sustain the family income during recessions.

Erdie Reynolds died at age 66 of an apparent heart attack in 1956, without knowing his son planned to join him in the family business after college, Doug Reynolds said.

Doug Reynolds returned as used car salesman and manager and then became general manager and owner. While people tried to take advantage of his youthfulness and inexperience, he immersed himself in the dealership and in community activities.

Most car dealerships were mom-and-pop businesses when Mr. Reynolds first started selling cars, he said. Showrooms were small in the early days. Car salesmen would stop to chat with people about their new cars. They would go to the country and talk with farmers in their fields or visit with factory workers after their workshifts ended, he said.

So much has changed in vehicle sales today, Doug Reynolds said. Customers often research the new models before coming into the showroom. The auto makers now control how cars are sold, he said.

Doug Reynolds promoted the auto industry through his community service. He was a trustee on the Black Hawk College board and helped develop a mechanics curriculum while serving on the advisory committee of United Township High School's Vocational Center. At one point, 11 Reynolds employees had received their training from the UT program, he said.

When Ford introduced its new models in 1961, Reynolds was one of five new car dealers with displays at the new car show at The Dock Restaurant in downtown Davenport.

By the mid-1960s, the Reynolds Co. had outgrown its downtown location in East Moline. After scouring several sites, Mr. Reynolds bought five acres along the former 42nd Avenue — now Avenue of the Cities — for a new showroom after 45 years in the same location.

The new showroom and service center, built in 1969, had six times the land and three times the building space with room to grow. The company now has almost 12 acres.

Doug Reynolds was elected in 1978 to the National Ford Dealers Council, representing more than 200 Ford dealerships in Chicago,

Minneapolis-St. Paul, Milwaukee, St. Louis and the Quad-Cities. He also co-chaired Ford's parts and service committee. Reynolds Co. was the first dealer in Illinois to have a Ford Motorcraft retail parts store.

Doug Reynolds, 72, recalls that cars sold for $1,900 when he first started selling them, and pickup trucks were not very popular.

Current sales are about half cars and half trucks, he said.

Vehicle sales are far more competitive today than ever before, as many foreign automakers pressure American sales, said Scott Reynolds, 45. New car and truck models have more standard features and select options than ever

Gary Krambeck / staff

Scott Reynolds, current owner of Reynolds Ford in East Moline, and father Doug Reynolds, owner-retired, celebrate the 75th anniversary of Reynolds Ford dealership as they stand in front of the new Ford GT and Ford Mustang in the dealership showroom in East Moline.

See ▶ Reynolds, F2

Scott and Doug featured in a story marking a third generation in the business.

CHAPTER NINE

God Sent Me
an Angel

AFTER MY WIFE'S PASSING, I pretty much sat around with my dog and just existed. Every night I would drink until I thought the pain and memories would disappear. It took about a month to figure out that this method of coping would not work for me. I could see no progress or healing. I knew it wasn't the answer.

I remember thinking about an old high school classmate I had who was an ex-mayor of East Moline. His wife had gone through a long illness and subsequent death. I saw him after she passed away at a mini reunion of locals. He looked great, alive, and he had a girlfriend. From what I could tell, he seemed to be doing more than okay. I called him and asked how he went from being in terrible shape after his wife died to being so normal and happy. His straightforward advice for me— "You've got to get out and be around people. You just have to."

After this conversation, I decided to call my deceased wife's best friend and tell her about it. She thought of someone she knew that she wanted to introduce me to that I could socialize with. So, I met her. She was a very nice lady. But it was like I was looking at my grandmother. I knew I would not go out with her again.

Another friend of mine had two gals in mind for me to meet. I met each of them with our mutual friends present. Unfortunately, I could tell right away that both would be a zero with me. I was very hung up on looks, and I just didn't feel any sort of attraction to these women.

I decided to go looking for companionship online. Apparently, there were several people that "matched" what I was looking for. I hoped to find someone who liked to play tennis, sail, was attractive, didn't have a lot of baggage, perhaps a widow themselves who was interested in meeting someone. I had several potentials online, but they were 200-300 miles away. My question for each was "How would you propose that we be able to get to know each other enough to go further with such a long distance between us?" Nobody could seem to answer this question with the exception of one gal. She said she would do anything, including move to wherever I wanted. She answered questions in a way that just seemed too good to be true. It turned out, she was. I saw one red flag after another in her responses. I found out later that the online dating service ended up banning her.

So now I am just disgusted with online dating and trying to meet someone in general. I took my dog for a walk and ended up stopping by my son's house. He lived somewhat close to me, and my path always went down his street and back. Scott was sitting outside, and we started talking. "Oh, by the way," he said, "Pam stopped by the dealership and she told me when you were ready to meet someone, she has just the person. And not to worry about being a gold-digger, she's got her own money."

Pam sold insurance plans to businesses. She called on us at the dealership, and apparently, she had known the person she wanted to introduce me to for many years. After Scott told me this, I went home and thought about it. It couldn't be any worse that what I currently had going on, so I gave Pam a call.

Pam told me about her friend. Her husband had passed away about four years prior, she was a fun, intelligent, and beautiful woman who spent time with her family, volunteering, and working in her own family business.

Ironically, her name was Donna.

I wanted to meet this new Donna.

Pam tried to set us up a few times with her and her husband, but the plans kept getting delayed. I asked if I could just call Donna myself. That's what I did.

When I called, she was working with her son and some light fixture reps, so she couldn't talk right then. I asked when I could call her back and she said she would be available to talk around 7:00 that evening.

I went about my typical routine. I fixed my dinner, sat around and watched television with my dog, and drank some beer. 7:00 finally came and I picked up the phone and gave Donna a call. It rang and rang and rang. I slammed the phone down and said "That bitch! I'm not gonna call her." I drank some more beer and at 9:00 I thought I should give her another chance. When she answered the phone, I immediately said, "Where were you?" She informed me that she had been home the entire time. I looked at the caller ID and realized that I had pushed one wrong number.

I can't believe she even agreed to see me after that.

I asked Donna if she would like to meet with me and see if there was anything there. We decided that I would come by her place to meet and we would have lunch at Jersey Grill. Her condo was near the restaurant.

When I arrived at her place, she opened the door and right away I thought, "This could be possible." Of course, I was basing this purely on her looks, but admittedly I could see there was something about how she looked and carried herself that I was attracted to.

We sat down on the couch together and she shared with me some photos of her family. I hate to admit this, but being the salesman that I am, I had prepared a packet to promote myself. After I looked at a few of her photos, I told her that I had some of my own in the car. I brought in my "packet" to show/sell her on me!

In this packet, I had a list of foods and music I like, and a huge photo of a beautiful sailboat that I own. I included that full-page photo of me in Time Magazine, a list of some of my awards, and I even brought a copy of my own obituary that I wrote myself. I had a bunch of comments attached to that from people and organizations that had nice things to say about me and how wonderful I was.

It was kind of comical, really. Even after that, she still wanted to have lunch with me. We headed out to Jersey Grill.

It was summertime and I was wearing a lightweight pair of pants. If I had my wallet in these pants, it would tend to pull them down, so I took money out of my wallet and put it in my pocket. We went inside, had a glass of beer and some BBQ. We had a really nice time. The conversation flowed naturally. We were getting ready to leave the restaurant and the skies started to open up and pour down rain. We stood by the door and couldn't even see my vehicle. Donna suggested we just stay and wait out the rain over a glass of wine.

She didn't know this, but without my wallet, I didn't have the money to pay for the wine. I had to ask her to pay for the wine on our first date! It didn't faze Donna a bit. It sort of became a joke after that.

After our first date, Donna agreed to get together with me again. From the list of my favorite foods I shared, we found out that we both like liver and onions. I suggested that I could fix that at my house and that's when a new pattern in my life began. We both had dogs; she would bring hers to my house when she visited me and I would cook, and the next weekend she would cook, and I would bring my dog along to her place.

Our dogs got to know each other. And so did we.

I wanted "this" Donna to be *my* Donna.

Donna had a quiet confidence about her. I saw this from the very first time we met on her doorstep. I didn't understand it at the time, but this draw that I had towards her went beyond physical attraction. It went deeper than that. She had an inner peace and happiness that I wanted.

This inner peace was God alive and at work in Donna's life. She let the Lord lead her life. For someone like me who was always striving and achieving in my own efforts, this concept was difficult to understand. But seeing it played out in Donna's life gave me an undeniable desire to want the same for myself.

God allowed me to come alive again through meeting Donna. I don't know why God would take her husband suddenly, and my wife as well. I don't understand how I could go to church my entire life but not really know the Lord.

But I do know that all the good things, the great things, and the terrible things that have happened in my life were all a part of God's plan for me to know him. I met him through a special angel—*my* Donna.

Doug and Donna

CHAPTER TEN
My Donna

SINCE MY FIRST and second wives both have the name "Donna," it might sound kind of confusing when I talk or write about my wife, "Donna." For the sake of clarity, I refer to my current wife as "my Donna."

I had a great life with my first wife. I was proud of her and was exposed to things that I never would have been had she not been in my life.

I feel the same way about my Donna right now. My Donna grew up in a small community on a dairy farm in Bemidji, Minnesota. Winters are pretty terrible there. When she was growing up, her family had fifty-nine-head of milk cows. That was a large number to have back then. Donna's father and her two brothers had to milk the cows twice a day, every day, no matter what the weather. It is pretty intense work. Her mother also worked on the farm, driving tractors, expecting help from Donna with all the meals and keeping the household organized.

Being remote and not in town, my Donna attended school in a one-room schoolhouse.

There weren't a lot of activities to participate in, not that she would have had time. However, she did take piano lessons and eventually assisted her teacher in teaching the younger students. My Donna played the violin in the school orchestra, and like me, was second chair. In her Senior. Year of high school, Donna worked at a rural electric association. She worked there every afternoon during her senior year in high school. After graduation she was offered a full-time position and continued working there until she married her first husband. She was promoted to receptionist and then Accounts Receivable Manager during this time.

WINTERS IN BEMIDJI, MINNESOTA

DONNA'S ONE-ROOM SCHOOLHOUSE

Donna continued to keep up with her responsibilities with the family farm as well. In between school, work, and family obligations, she maintained friendships with people in the neighborhood and her friends at school. On weekends, my Donna would spend time with her friends and go to barn dances. That is where she met her first husband. He was in the service and would attend dances when he came back. When they talked about getting married, he wanted to go back to the farm, but she said, "no way!"

BAND AT A BARN DANCE

Donna, her husband, and her brothers had heard of electrical contracting jobs in Mount Pleasant, Iowa. They made the move to live and work for an electric company. When work became slow in Mount Pleasant, Donna and her husband came to Davenport to work for an uncle who owned Shaw Electric.

After a few years, Donna's brothers wanted them to come back to Mount Pleasant, as the owners of the company they had previously worked for were selling. They went back and the three of them together bought Mount Pleasant Electric. They successfully ran that company for thirty-six years. Donna and her husband raised their two sons and a daughter in Mount Pleasant.

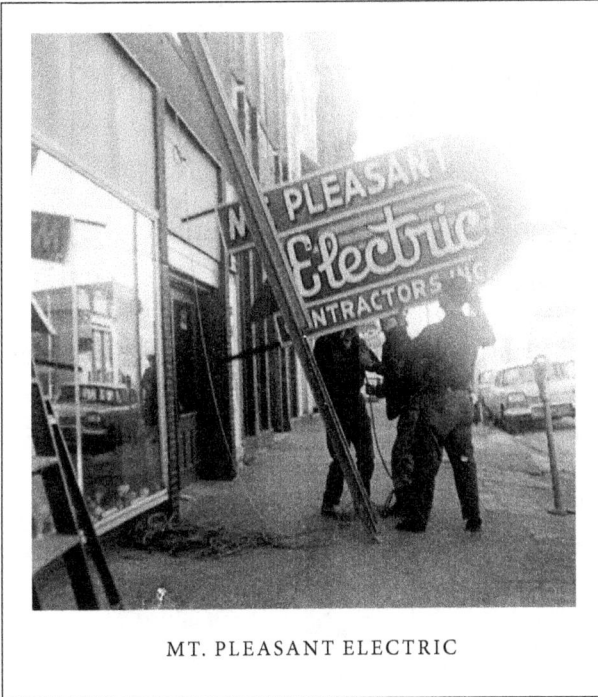

MT. PLEASANT ELECTRIC

They built a house on a five-acre lake. They had 100 acres total and the kids grew up hunting, trapping and really had a wonderful life in Mount Pleasant. I don't know how Donna did it all, but she was an excellent mother and an excellent wife.

When the children were all in school, Donna went to work at Production Credit which was an organization that lent large sums of money to farmers, financing their crops and livestock. She worked there for 19 years, working her way up to become the Administrative Assistant to the President of the company, which also included overseeing 3 branch offices.

DONNA'S HOME IN MT. PLEASANT, IOWA

After the kids were out of college, the owner of Shaw Electric in Davenport approached them about selling his business. Donna, her husband, and both sons bought him out, and they moved back to this area. Because of the economy and high interest rates the business was pretty small when they took it over. There were only a couple of electricians employed at the time. With the new ownership, Shaw Electric soon began to thrive and grow to support over 100 electricians.

When things started to look better for the Shaw business, Donna wanted to open up a store called "Light Expressions." This was before Menards and other stores sold interior lights. So, if you were a builder, you had to specifically shop for lights at a lighting store. Light Expressions by Shaw was extremely successful. Donna had won trips overseas, she visited China to see what the fixtures were made of, and really threw herself into this work.

During this time, in order to bid on certain jobs, businesses had to have a minority owner. Shaw Electric didn't have that, so Donna went out and bought an electrical business in the small town of Durant, Iowa, and used that license in order to get minority contracts. I think that was just genius.

Donna decided to expand Light Expressions and opened a store in Iowa City. She also heard of a store in Des Moines that was going broke. She went there on her own, found a new strip mall in Waukee, and opened a state-of-the-art lighting store. She kept the store for five years before selling it. After she sold that store, the next owner went broke. She eventually ended up selling all of her stores because recently Menards, other big box stores, and internet sales, were diluting business for the specialty stores. It was painful for Donna as Light Expressions by Shaw had been her baby.

It was quite the place to buy lighting and fixtures. That is where I bought mine when I built a house. Of course, I didn't know her then.

Accent your home with lighting

Light fixtures are no longer just simple lamps. Today's trends include multi-colored chandeliers, cobalt glass and eclectic lamp shades.

Press-Citizen / Deb Barber

Leslie Bohlen, left, and Donna Shaw of Light Expressions By Shaw in Coralville demonstrate how light fixtures now come in families to coordinate lighting, art and furniture for an entire room.

DONNA AT LIGHT EXPRESSIONS

Shaw Electric is their family's main business now. It is primarily commercial and industrial contracting and is run by Donna's two sons. Some of her grandchildren have also joined the business.

I wasn't a part of my Donna's life when she grew up, married, built a business, raised children and all of that. But these things helped shape who she is today.

I'm awfully proud to be a part of her life today.

It didn't take long for me to know that I wanted Donna to be my wife. We continued to meet at each other's homes for dinner. Racing back and forth across the river in the winter made things a little harder. I could tell we both were thinking the same thing, so I asked Donna if she would marry me. She agreed.

It then became a situation where I was wondering how to tell her sons that I wanted to marry their mother. We all knew each other from family functions and such, but getting married is different than inviting me to a grandchild's birthday party.

Donna and I went to their family business. Donna needed to talk to the accountant anyway, so we went together, and I hoped to be able to talk to her boys, Bob and Steve. After some small talk in Steve's office, I finally got around to asking the question: "What would you boys say if I told you that your mother and I were going to get married?"

One of Donna's boys turned and looked out the window. I believe his response was something like "That's impossible."

The other son asked me how long we had even known each other. I know in my heart that God gave me the words to say because I am just not bright enough to think of this on my own. I replied, "It's not about how long we've known each other; it's about how much time we have left together." That statement seemed to diffuse the situation, but I could tell that Donna's sons still weren't convinced that we should marry.

Soon after we met that day in Steve's office, they accepted me as a part of the family.

We had a formal ceremony in the British Virgin Islands and brought thirty-four members of our family, including our children, grandchildren and siblings, to witness and celebrate. The week prior to our wedding in the British Virgin Islands, we held a private ceremony at Bettendorf Christian Church to eliminate the rules of being married out of the country.

We purchased a home a few months prior to our wedding and Donna and I redecorated the home we bought together to make it our own. When we were at the closing and taking possession of the house, I was handed one key and the garage door opener. The rest of the keys were in the house. I told Donna to take the key and wait by the front door. I used the garage door opener to go in and come around. I wanted to carry her across the threshold. I thought it was a romantic idea—an idea that quickly turned comedic.

After the first try of picking her up, I said, "You're going to have to kind of hop," and in my attempt to catch her in my arms as she hopped into them, I took a step, my knee gave out, and I ended up throwing Donna through the door. I cut my arm on the door jamb as I fell on top of her. We both laid on the floor laughing.

It was a fun start to our life together. We have been having fun and laughing ever since.

For our formal ceremony, Donna and I each made reservations for our family members to come with us to the British Virgin Islands. I remember many nights of Donna sitting at her computer, me at mine, while we coordinated the travel details together, purchasing airline tickets, etc.

Donna and I arrived the evening before everyone else. We had some time to meet with the people at the resort and pick out a cake, make arrangements for the girls to have their hair done and things like that. We also had the boat brought around and dock towards the front of where the reception was to be held. When our family started to arrive, we had hors d'oeuvres for everyone and they were all welcome to check out my sailboat.

The next day we were married by a pool with an archway set up. Donna's three granddaughters were her attendants, and my son, Scott was my best man. When Donna came around the corner, I just shook my head and thought, "Wow." We wrote our own vows and were sure to bring God into them. We wanted to do this because we knew that God had brought us together. Every circumstance we both faced, all of the chances we could have had to meet earlier and didn't, everything about our lives, both separate, and now together, all pointed to God. That is why we included this as a part of our wedding vows to each other. Donna's grandson, Matt, married us.

Following the wedding, we celebrated on the docks. The tables and chairs were all covered in white with large light blue bows. The napkins were light blue. It was appropriately nautical and beautiful.

I continue to appreciate my Donna for what a wonderful and good person she is—a person of God—and how lucky I am that God brought us together. He knew what he was doing, that's for sure. We are both happier than we have ever been. I don't mean this to be a negative comment towards my first wife or towards Donna's first husband. There is some natural history there and neither one of us can deny that our lives prior to meeting were good.

But I know we are both grateful to have a life together. We are so compatible. It's funny to think about how both of our roots were from far different places. She grew up on a farm, and I in the city. Our respective businesses, although both successful, also had different beginnings.

We agree on most everything. We simply get along. There is no discord. If there is a disagreement, it doesn't fester or become something larger than what it should be. We find ways to solve any issues without being hurtful and without trying to stand up for our own position. It's kind of like the Bible says in the passage about love in First Corinthians. Our love is patient, kind, it isn't jealous, rude, self-seeking, or easily angered. Our love does not delight in evil but rejoices with the truth. It protects, trusts, hopes, and perseveres.

We are so blessed.

Celebrating our wedding in the British Virgin Islands

CHAPTER ELEVEN
Spiritual Awakening

A S I FIRST GOT TO KNOW DONNA, I was also getting to know God through her. There was this mystique trait that she had, and I just didn't understand what it was. I could see it in her feelings towards others and how she approached every aspect of her life. She would say things like, "I guess God has a plan," and I would nod and wonder what that really meant. I started recognizing that she had a deep and genuine faith that I didn't have, even though I attended church myself.

Donna's faith intrigued me. I wanted what she had. It seemed that I had been striving my whole life for things, and when I got what I wanted, I didn't experience the satisfaction that I had hoped for, so I was constantly on to the next goal. I even remember my first wife asking me why I would join all the committees and chair all the things that I did. I just wanted to do something good with my life. I know I did good things, but I never found that feeling of satisfaction.

I recognized this in Donna. She had a very successful career of her own, but she didn't have this clamoring to climb the next rung. She was satisfied and the reason for that was because she believed God was running her life, not herself.

We attended church services together, one week at her church, then the next week at a church I started attending after my wife passed away. Eventually we decided on one church in Bettendorf where her grandson was a pastor.

I started having these experiences when we attended church together. At the time, I didn't know what to call them, but now I know that these experiences were the Holy Spirit speaking to my heart.

One of these times was during a baptism service. There was this sort of dunk-tank that they used right there in the church. I had watched people get baptized and I would clap for them. But one Sunday there wasn't anyone being baptized. I leaned over and told Donna that I wanted to be baptized. She thought that was a good thing, that I was ready. I contacted her grandson, Matt, and he said he would baptize me wherever I wanted. I got to thinking that I didn't want to do it in front of the church, so maybe we could do it in the Mississippi.

After that, I kept wanting to hear God's voice or recognize clearly that He was the one leading me to do things in my life. One of these "clear messages" came when I felt God leading me to reconnect with my old high school buddy, John. John was the best man in my first wedding, and I hadn't seen him in years. He was kind of crippled up from football and wrestling in college. He was experiencing other health issues too. When his wife passed away, I felt like I should contact him. John wasn't going to church and Donna and I got him to start going. Now he attends regularly, and when we meet to do something like go shooting (something John loves to do), he will ride in the car and say, "Look at this day that God has provided for." I'm glad I followed God's leading in getting in touch with John.

Another time that God made a real spiritual impression on me was when I went on a men's retreat with Donna's son. I felt somewhat obligated to go because he was a Deacon in his church, and since he asked me, I thought I should go.

Just before the retreat, Donna and I were in Mexico. Before we left, I had found a Bible in our room, so we opened it and began reading. I don't remember what the passages were, but when I arrived at the men's retreat later that same day, the very first reading we had was the exact one Donna and I had read in Mexico. I knew this was more than just a coincidence—that it was a God thing. I was really humbled that God cared enough for me to know that these promptings and coincidences were hand-picked for me.

Another example is a little more recent. One Sunday in church they held a special offering for missions. The sermon was very good and was on the topic of "have you given enough?" When the offering came around, I reached in and pulled out a hundred-dollar bill. But as I sat there waiting for the basket to come, I kept thinking, *is this going all out? Am I giving everything?* A hundred dollars is a lot for a special offering. But as the basket came, I just put in all the money I had in my wallet. I don't look for praise for this. I'm only sharing because I felt a real connection with God that I should do it.

A similar thing with money happened with our church building program. The church was campaigning for pledges and I committed to giving $10,000. I thought that was a good amount to donate. I followed up with the church, wondering when the building was going to start. I was put off when I found out that they wouldn't begin until later. I again felt the need to do more because I could afford to do more. I felt like I needed to stretch to the point of being uncomfortable and give to the point where it was not easy to do so.

Again, I don't like to talk about monetary amounts as examples of my growing faith, but these amounts were God-given. They were not to glorify me by any means.

I had a real hunger to learn and grow in my faith. Another stretching experience was at a retreat I went with Donna's grandson. I remember hearing people from our church talk about getting involved in small groups and having accountability. I hadn't connected with a whole lot of people in the church at this time, but this retreat definitely changed that for me.

A professional basketball athlete-turned minister was the guest speaker at this retreat. He talked about when the team is in a huddle and the coach is telling you what to do, the team builds camaraderie by leaning in. Everyone in the huddle is leaning in to the coach. This speaker talked about how we need to do this as a church. The illustration really resonated with me.

I told Donna that I wanted to be more intentional about getting to know people at church. My habit had been to go to church and leave right after. I wanted to meet people and lean in. We decided to start going a little early.

In the church vestibule there are tables and chairs for people to gather and visit. I now make a point to get better acquainted with people. I believe that associating with other Christians is what I need to do and what God wants me to do.

I have this devotional that I'm reading that Donna gave me. It's called *Jesus Calling*. I also study a daily prayer guide called *Face to Face* that gives me a deeper look into many aspects communing with God. I pick these up and read them every day. If I don't do that, I don't feel right. Donna and I also attend a weekly bible study that consists of extensive homework, small group discussion, and a lecture for the whole group. We are in the midst of planning a family trip to Israel. Even though Donna and I have independently been to Israel, we feel the need of a deeper spiritual experience that only the Holy Land can deliver. We also feel fortunate to have Donna's grandson, Matt, who is a Chaplain in the Army, and her son, Bob, who is a Deacon in the Catholic church to be our "spiritual leaders" on this trip.

I'm still on this big journey when it comes to my faith. I know I'm not anywhere close to "there." But I truly want to share what I have with my children, grandchildren, and all of their spouses. I am involved in apologizing to my kids for the things I have done wrong—another step in my faith journey. I want to try and bring them closer to each other, to me, and to God.

Epilogue

THE VERY FIRST LINE of this book is about how I've written my own obituary. Now I can say that I've written my own book. It is my desire that the words written will be more than just some family history, but a dialogue of how my life has changed throughout history.

I'm sure that everyone has heard the cliché about how money isn't everything, or how money can't buy you happiness. These sayings are true. I cannot deny the benefits that have come to me because of success in life, work, and finances. But I've concluded that nothing compares to the peace I've experienced from growing closer in relationship to my creator—God.

I've shared some of the things I consider "highlights" of my life. There are so many extremely magical things that I've done and experienced that I even included some bullet points in some of the chapters in case someone reads those and wants to ask me about them. I could go on and on about the glitz and glory in my life.

But the thing I really want you to see, the things I really want people to ask me about is my faith. I want all of those I love to experience the benefits of putting their faith in God.

Now more than ever, I am aware that I just won't be around forever. When I am gone from this earth, I hope that people will say nice things about me. But at the end of the day and at the end of my life, the only thing that really matters is what God says about me.

I know I'm forgiven and saved by grace. I know that Jesus died on the cross with my sins on his back. I know that he loves me. None of this happened by my own efforts or strength—two things I've relied on nearly all of my life.

I also know when I leave this world that my family will be taken care of. Another thing I have worked hard for. Another gift allowed to me by God.

My biggest regret in life is not providing my family a foundation of faith to build on from early on. But I've learned in my later years that it is never too late to experience the peace that comes from knowing God. I know it may sound strange for my children and grandchildren to hear their grandpa pray at meals or talk about matters of faith. It's important to me. They are important to me.

More than anything, I want my family, friends, and anyone who reads this to have what I have—peace, salvation, a relationship with God, and an eternity in heaven.

Sooner or later we all will submit to God. If you do it now, I think you will be much happier. Your external circumstances may not change; but your outlook on life in light of eternity will.

I like to tell stories. If you've sat with me or have read this far, then that is probably clear to you. But sometimes I feel inadequate in my ability to truly express my faith and how it means so much more to me than the other stories I tell. It's hard to describe peace from God to someone who hasn't experienced it themselves. I want what I share to be more than just words. I want it to be personal.

That is why I am using the final words in this book to address some personal notes to my family. If you have read this far, then I want you to know that I've prayed for you and I love you. And if you haven't already met the Lord, I hope my story was a good introduction to Him.

Blessings

To My Children and Grandchildren:

I apologize for not letting you know the Lord and experience how wonderful his perfect peace and love can make you feel. I pray that you will all someday accept HIM into your lives. Please forgive me for this and for not knowing how to properly express how much I love you all. I want to say it over and over—I love you.

To My Daughter, Sherri:

What a wonderful person you are. What a wonderful teacher you have become. You also are a good athlete. Your willingness to help others in both your work and in your personal life is extremely special. It is my hope that you will continue on a path to know Christ better. I love you. I am proud of the person you have become. I believe with all of my heart that you will find a new level of happiness that comes from really knowing Jesus.

To My Son, Scott:

Along with your natural mischievousness, you have shown an incredible ability to be really good at the many activities that interest you; including selling vehicles and closing deals, working on your house, training and raising your dogs, as well as your fishing ability. Scott, you are a wonderful father and I am so proud of you. My prayer for you is that you will one day allow GOD to lead your life and that you will experience the lifting of all of your burdens when you give them over to HIS help. I pray you will trust HIM with your happiness and that HE will bring to you a Christian woman to share your life with.

To My Granddaughter, Suni:

You have all kinds of talent! You have shown this at every job you have ever had. God blessed you with two wonderful children who I am sure will contribute to the world in special ways. Always remember to be the parent that shows them how special they are. It is my desire that you, August, and Avery will get to know Jesus in an intimate way, and that the three of you will follow GOD'S plan for your lives.

To My Grandson, Bill:

What can I say about all you have accomplished and the person you have become? You not only have a natural ability to teach and draw out the best in your students, but you give each of them an example of confidence, discipline, and excellence. My hope for you is that you would get deeply reacquainted with GOD and that you will raise your children to know HIM. There is no greater joy and no greater achievement than this.

To My Granddaughter, Carolyn:

What an amazing talent for both athletics and nursing you possess. You have worked hard to achieve a level of excellence. I pray you will come to know that GOD is the one who gave you the gifts and abilities you have. Please allow God into your life on a regular basis. I know HE can and will lead you into even greater paths. I know that we aren't always in sync with God's timing, but be patient, granddaughter. I know he will lead you on to more than you can imagine.

To My Granddaughter, Lexy:

Your true beauty, brains, and the drive to accomplish great things are gifts from God. I pray you will acknowledge GOD as your maker and giver of good things. I just look at all you have done in a short amount of time and am proud of you. You are like me, I think, in that you haven't always thought of GOD as being the one to help you on your journey. It wasn't until recently that I came to this realization about GOD and how HE has allowed me to attain a magical and blessed life.

My hope is that you will recognize GOD and follow HIM as he leads you to a greater path of happiness and accomplishments.

To My Grandson, Jon:

How brilliant you are! You are an easy example of the proof that there is a GOD and what HE can provide for you. GOD gave you an incredible intelligence. From an early age, you were unhappy with the level of learning in school and sought a higher level. My hope for you is that you will recognize that GOD gave you this gift and you will follow His path in how you apply it in your future.

To My Grandson, Jack:

And how brilliant you are! God clearly created you with the ability to create. You possess a rare talent of reproducing images in paint, pencil, and other mediums that amaze me! GOD gave you the ability to bring color and expression through your artistic works. I pray God will give you the confidence and happiness you need and that you will follow HIM as you share your talent with the world. Please allow yourself to follow HIM.

To My Great-Grandchildren, August and Avery:

Your young life is just beginning, but GOD has afforded both of you with incredible intelligence. Use it wisely and you will achieve marvelous things. Get to know Jesus and God and you will experience things at a higher level. Only with HIM can you attain the unimaginable.

To all of you reading these words:

*"Now to him who is able to do immeasurably more
than all we ask or imagine,
according to his power that
is at work within us,
to him be glory in the church
and in Christ Jesus
throughout all generations,
for ever and ever!*

Amen"

Ephesians 3:20-21 (NIV)

About the Author

Douglas Reynolds has truly loved the Lord, his wives, his children, and his Terrier dogs. He has enjoyed all sports, but especially tennis and sailing on the Donna J. Douglas's greatest desire is that others will get to know the Lord and receive His peace in their lives. Please remember this life-changing event after reading my story and "God's Plan."

www.ingramcontent.com/pod-product-compliance
Lightning Source LLC
Chambersburg PA
CBHW071602040426
42452CB00008B/1257